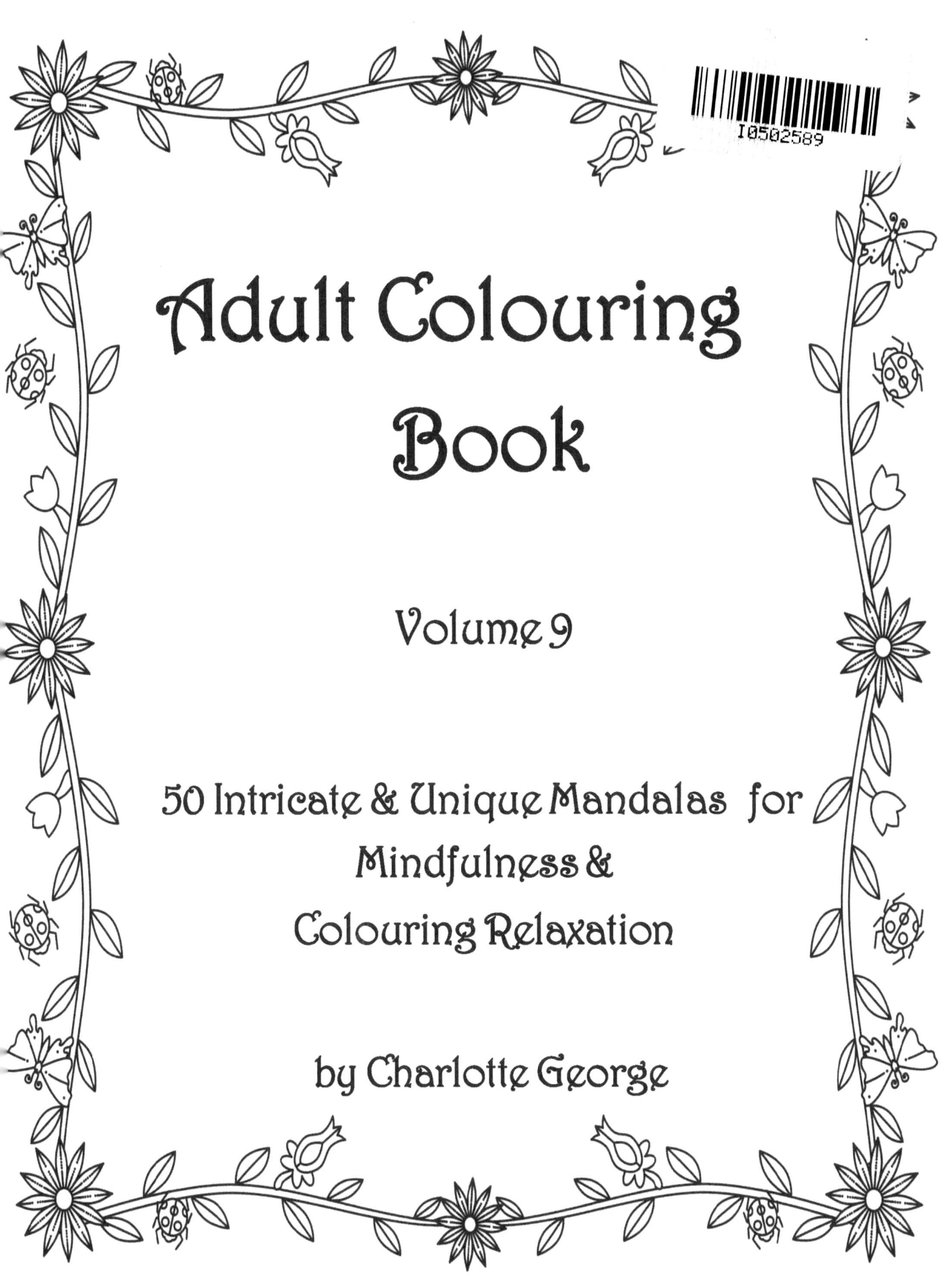

Adult Colouring Book

Volume 9

50 Intricate & Unique Mandalas for
Mindfulness &
Colouring Relaxation

by Charlotte George

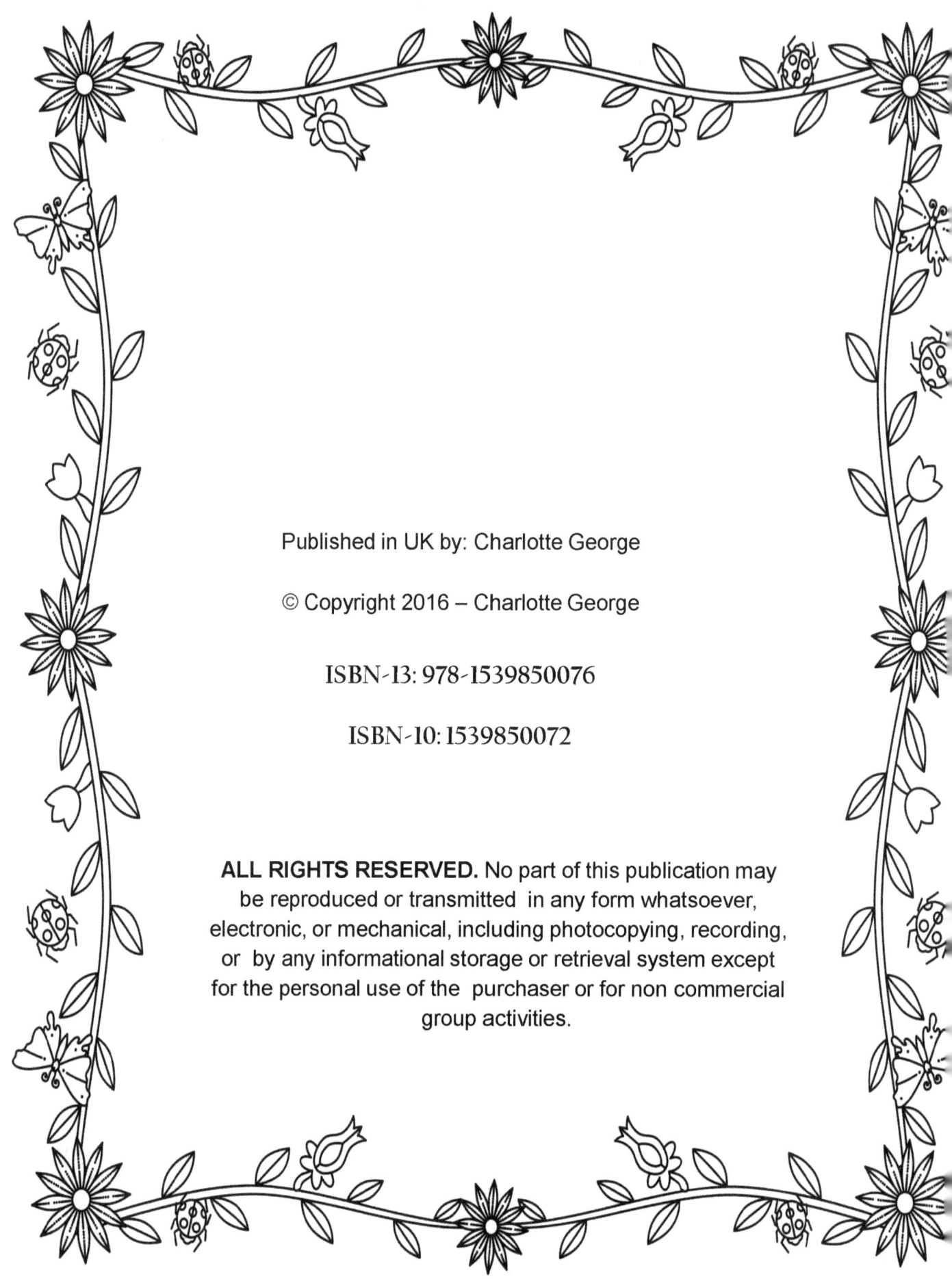

Published in UK by: Charlotte George

© Copyright 2016 – Charlotte George

ISBN-13: 978-1539850076

ISBN-10: 1539850072

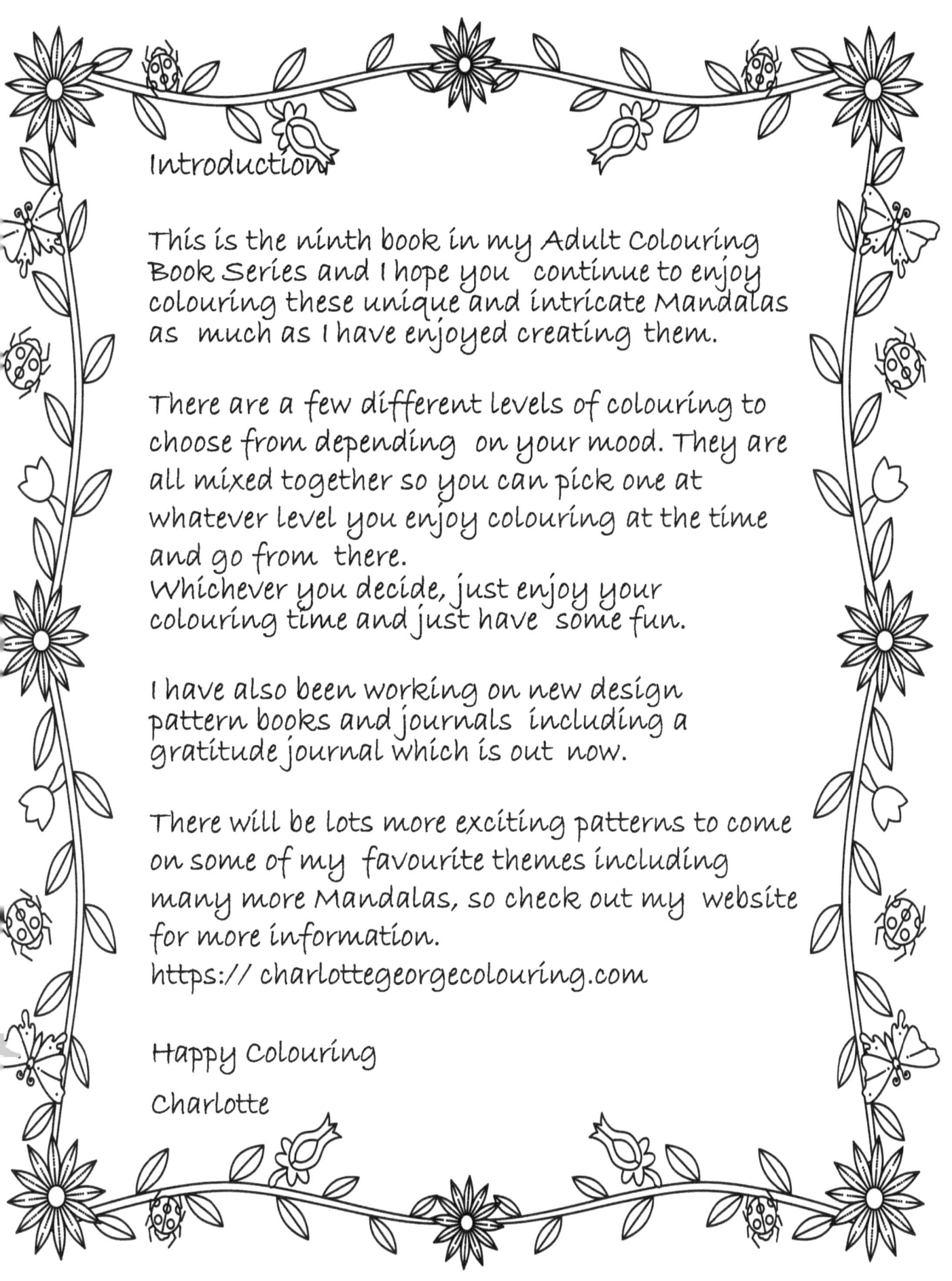

Introduction

This is the ninth book in my Adult Colouring Book Series and I hope you continue to enjoy colouring these unique and intricate Mandalas as much as I have enjoyed creating them.

There are a few different levels of colouring to choose from depending on your mood. They are all mixed together so you can pick one at whatever level you enjoy colouring at the time and go from there.
Whichever you decide, just enjoy your colouring time and just have some fun.

I have also been working on new design pattern books and journals including a gratitude journal which is out now.

There will be lots more exciting patterns to come on some of my favourite themes including many more Mandalas, so check out my website for more information.
https:// charlottegeorgecolouring.com

Happy Colouring

Charlotte

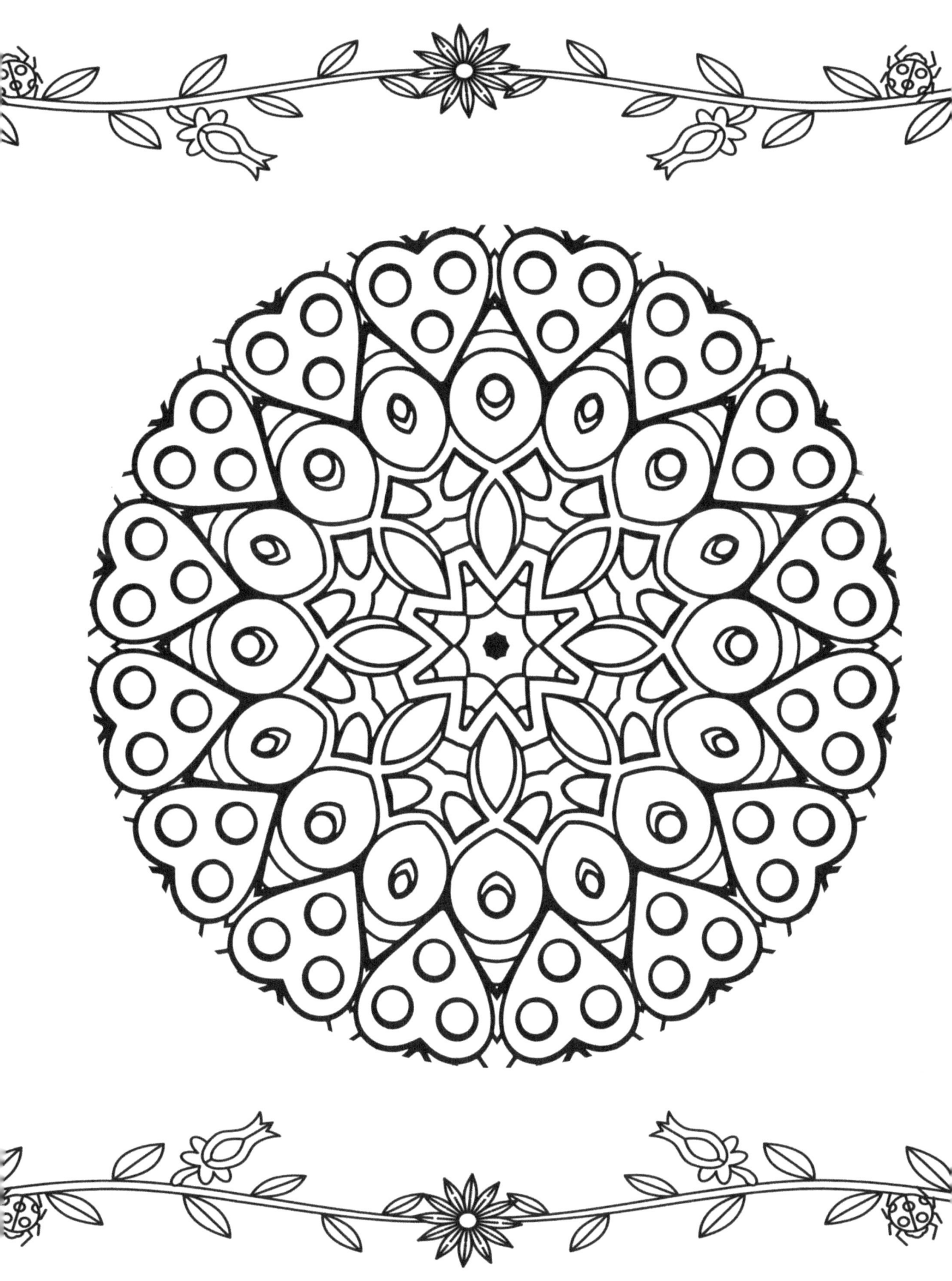

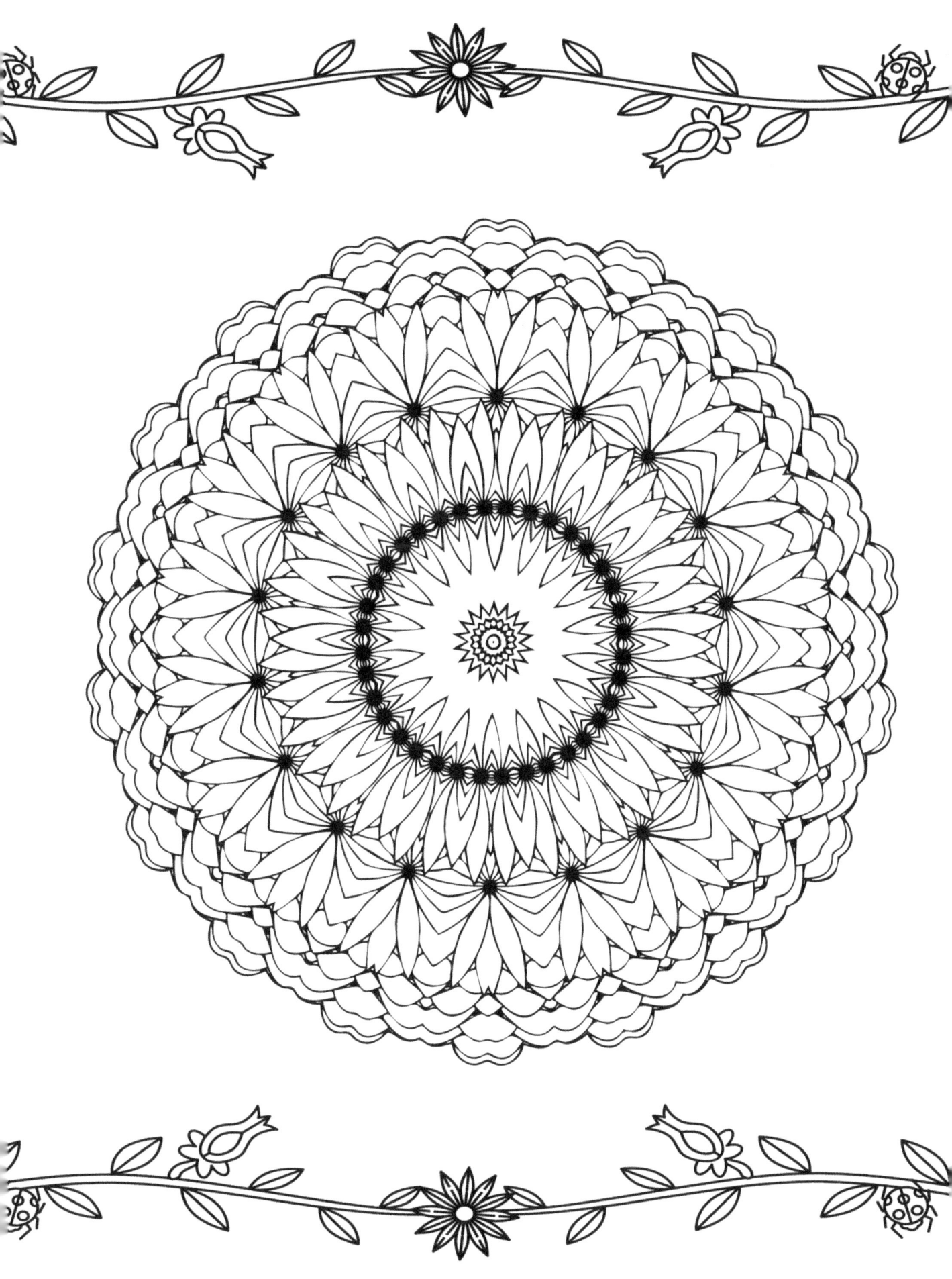

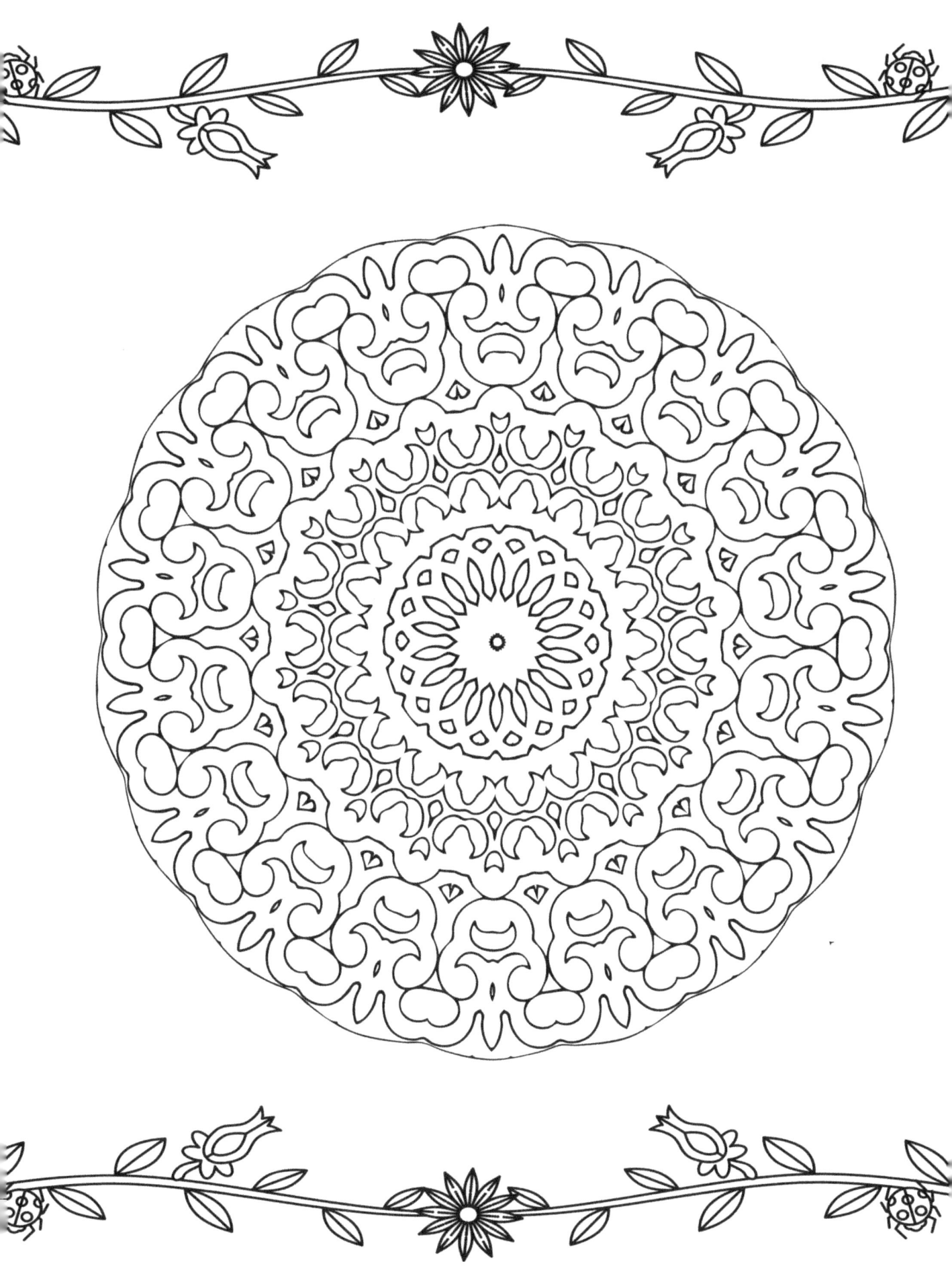

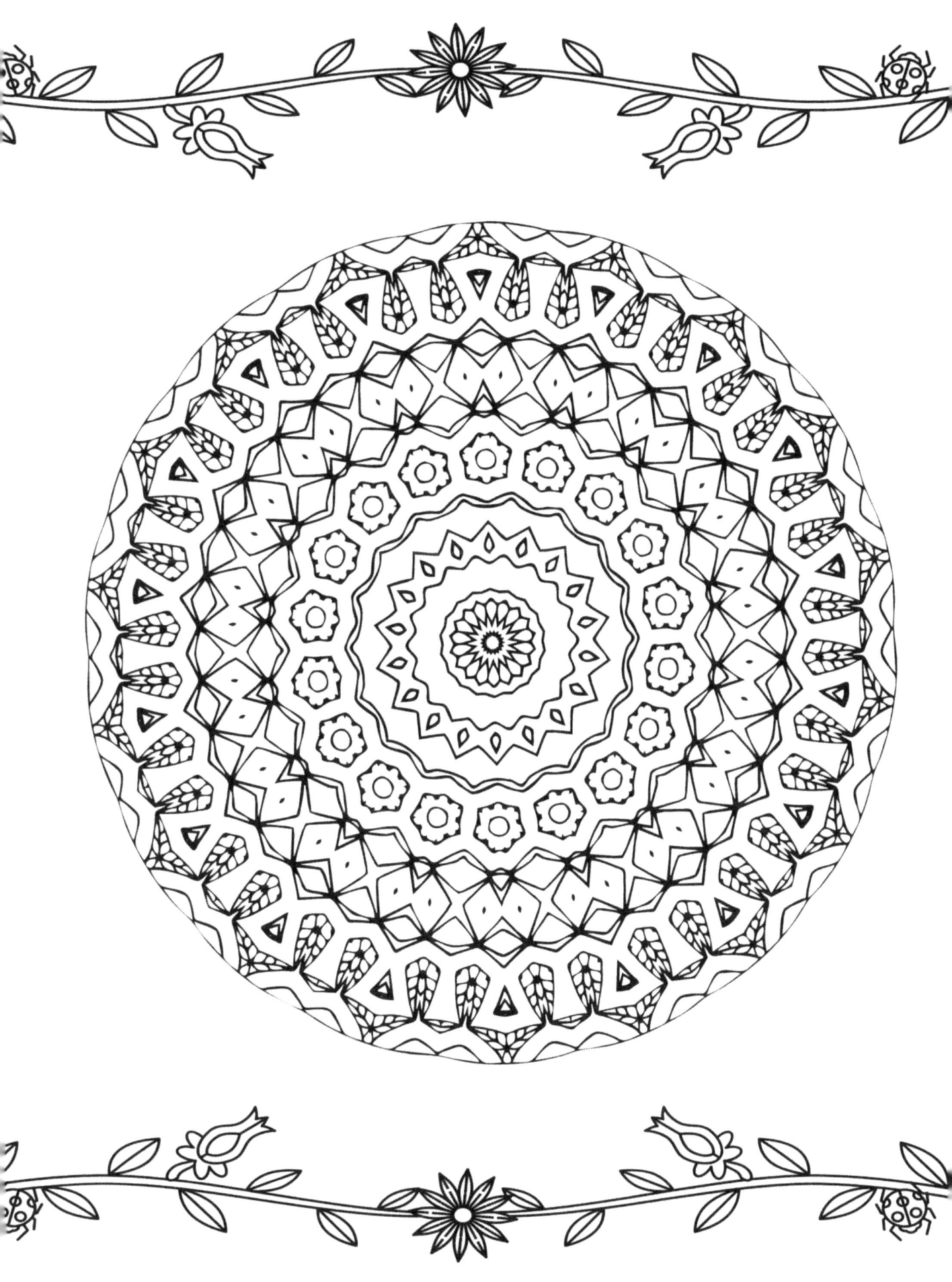

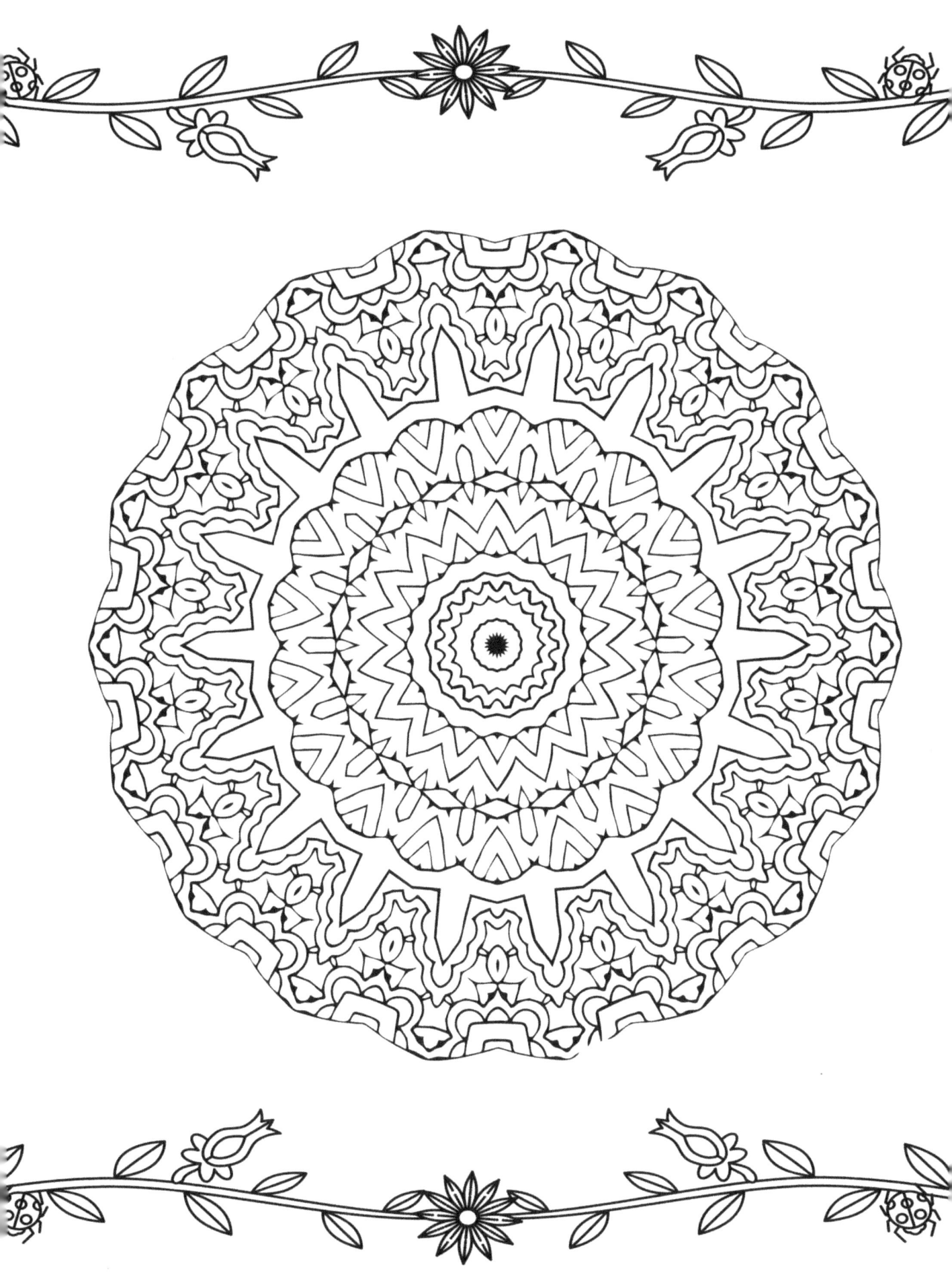

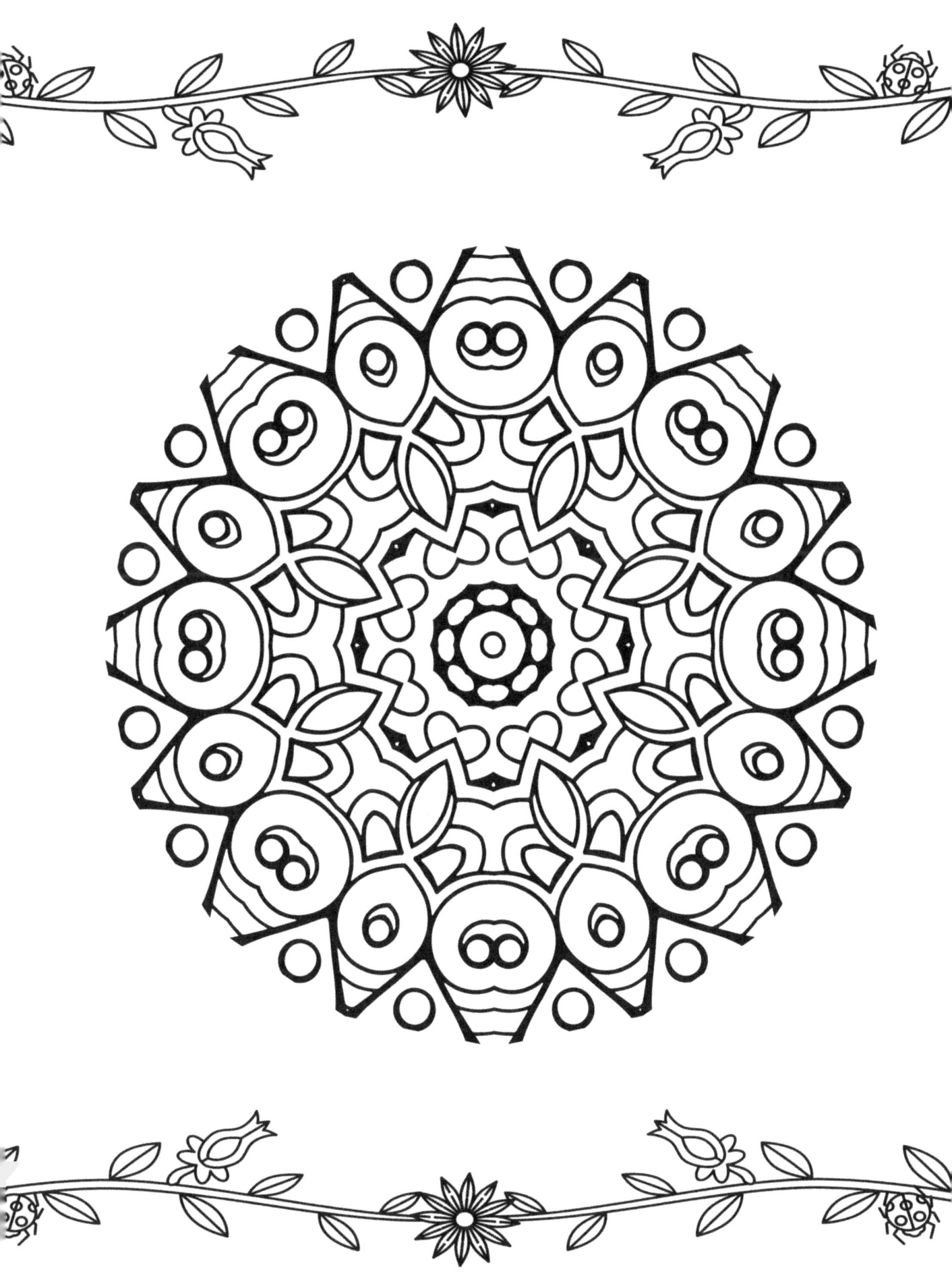

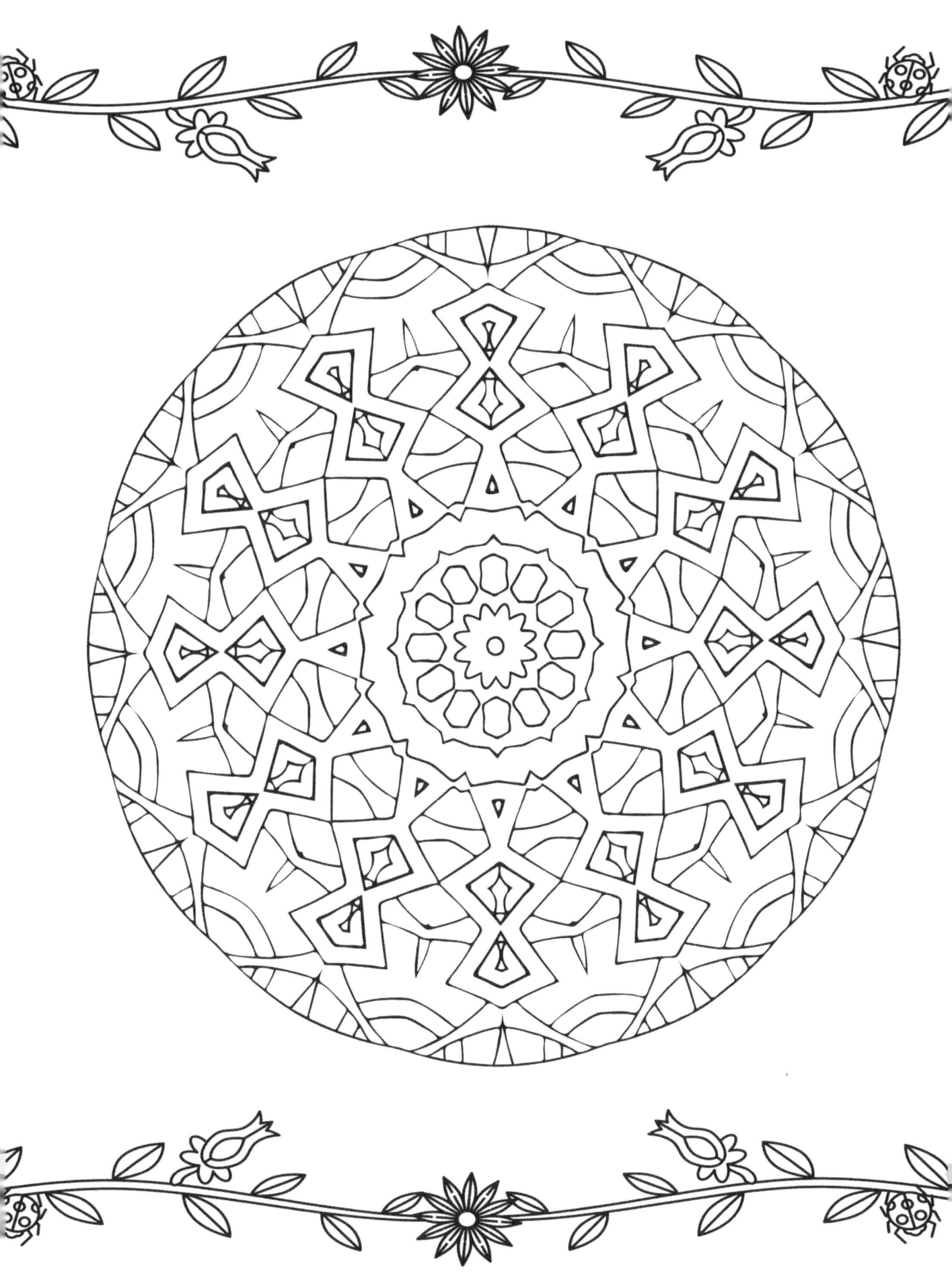

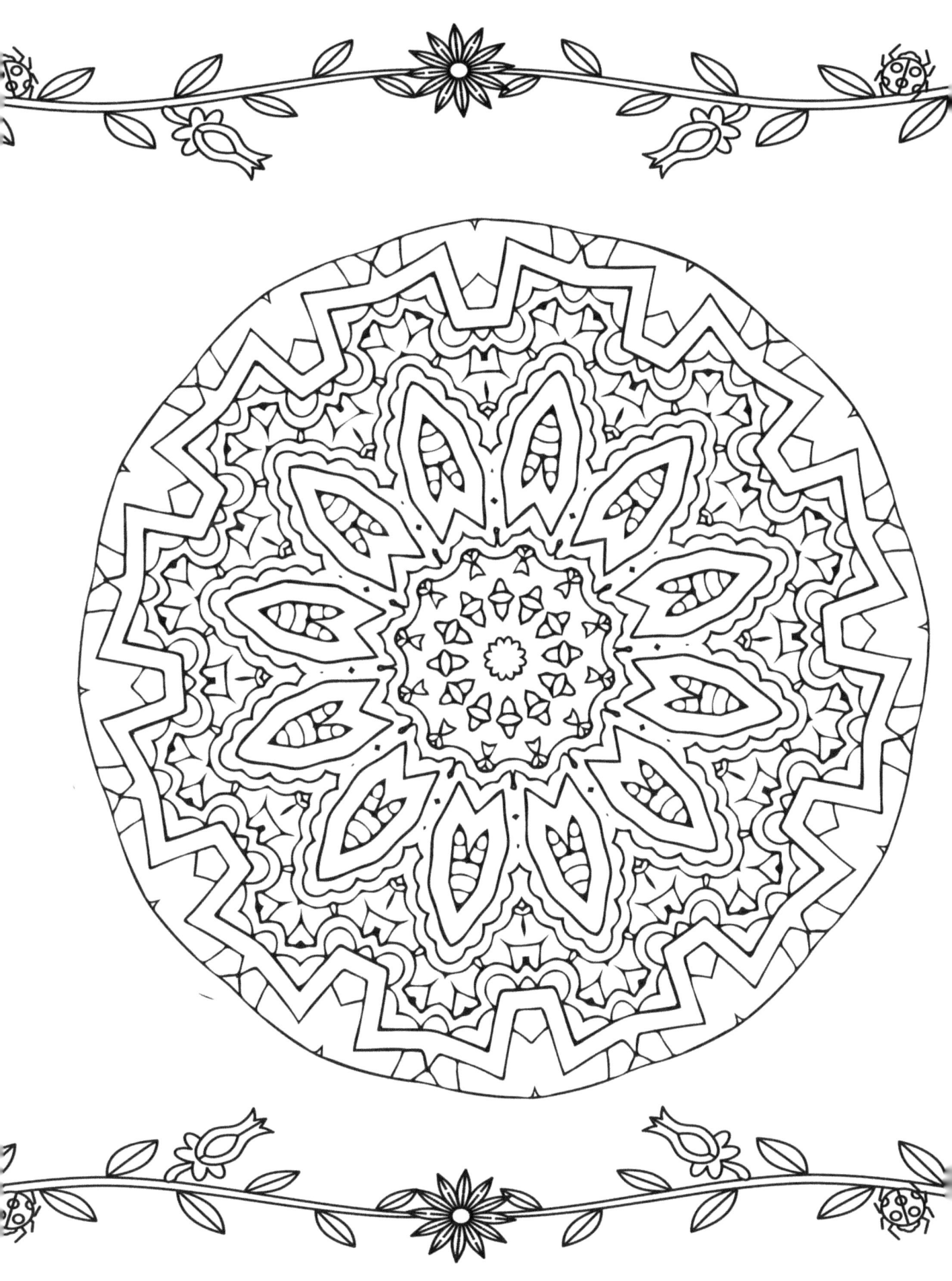

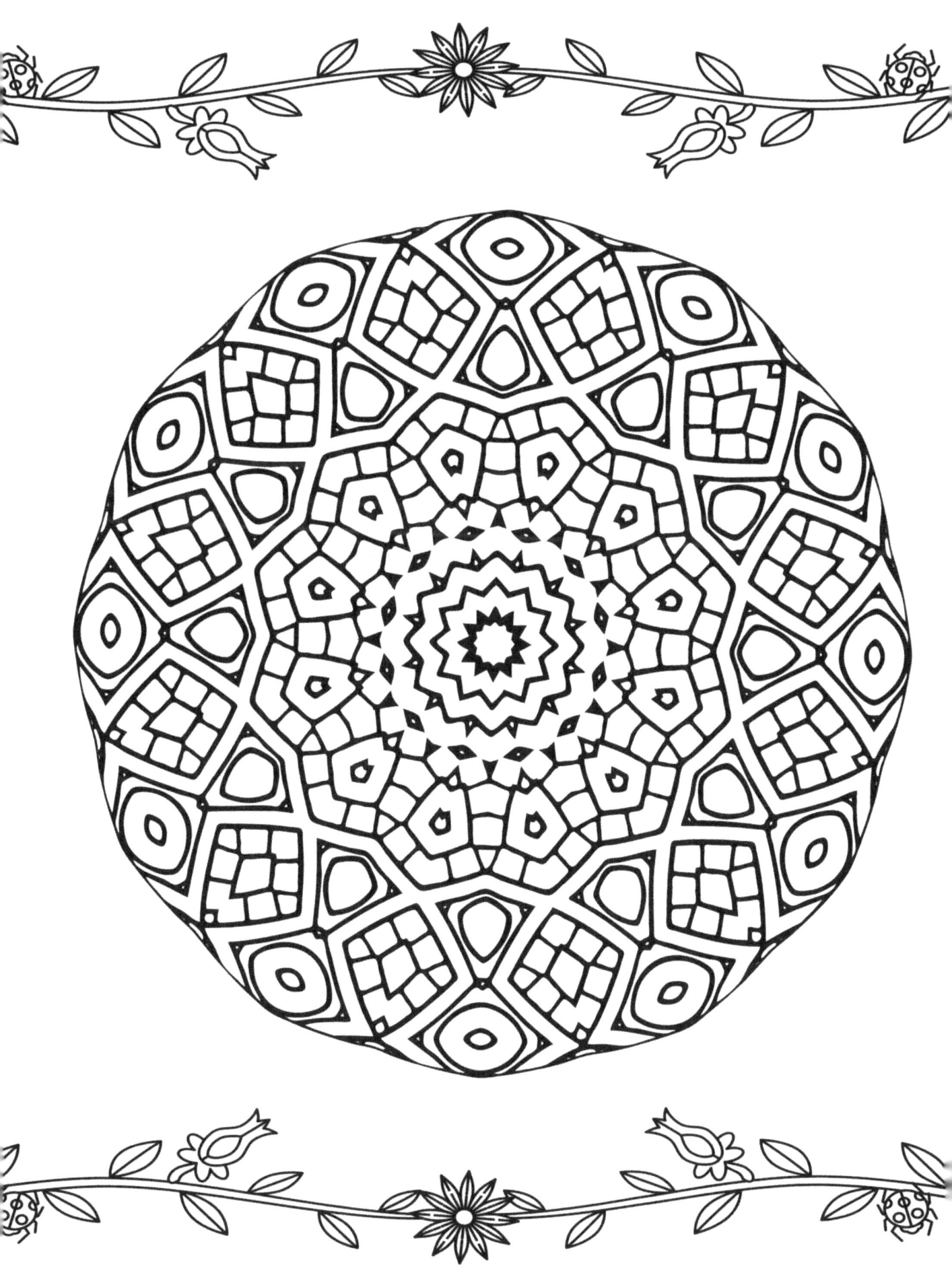

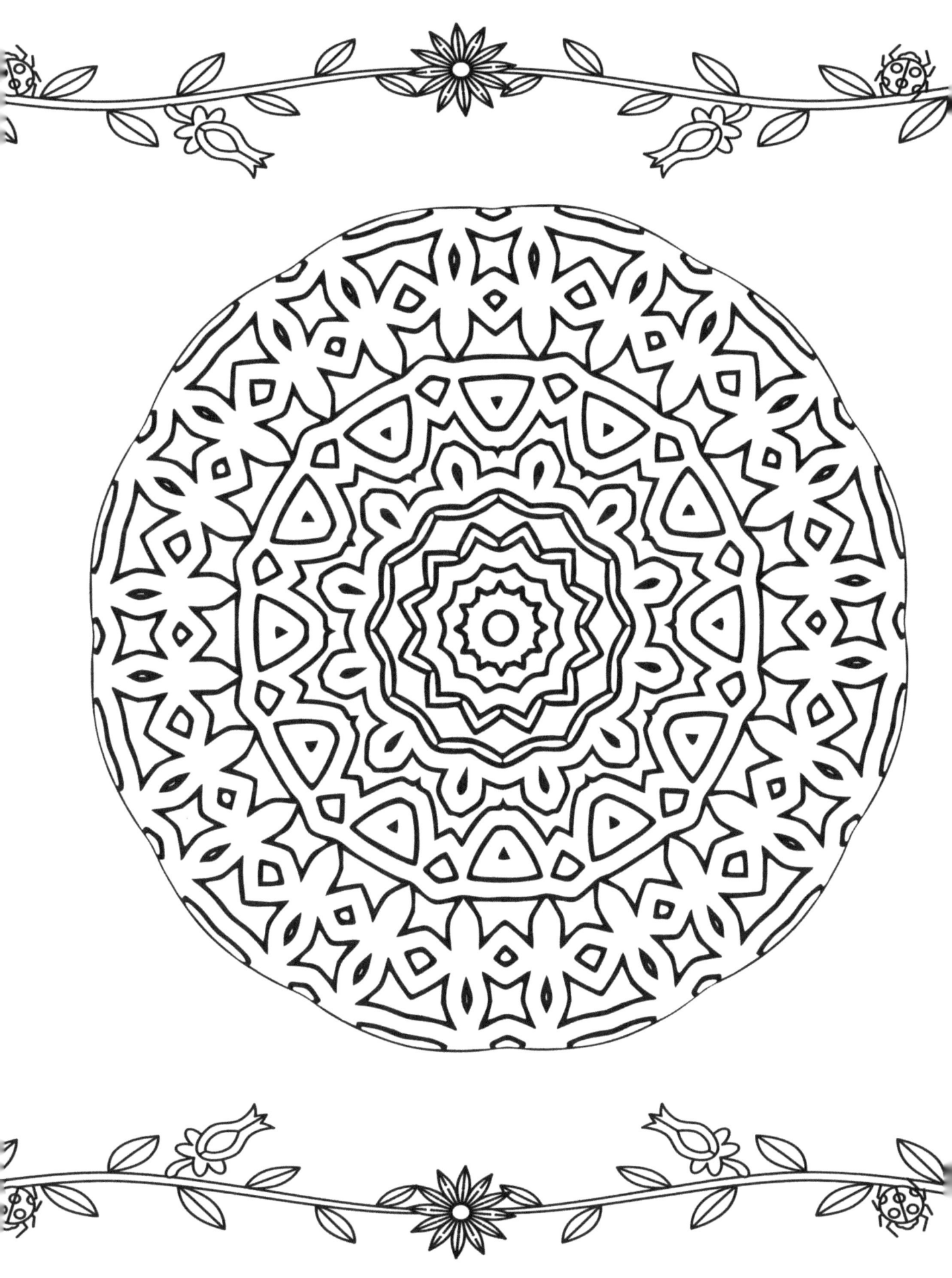

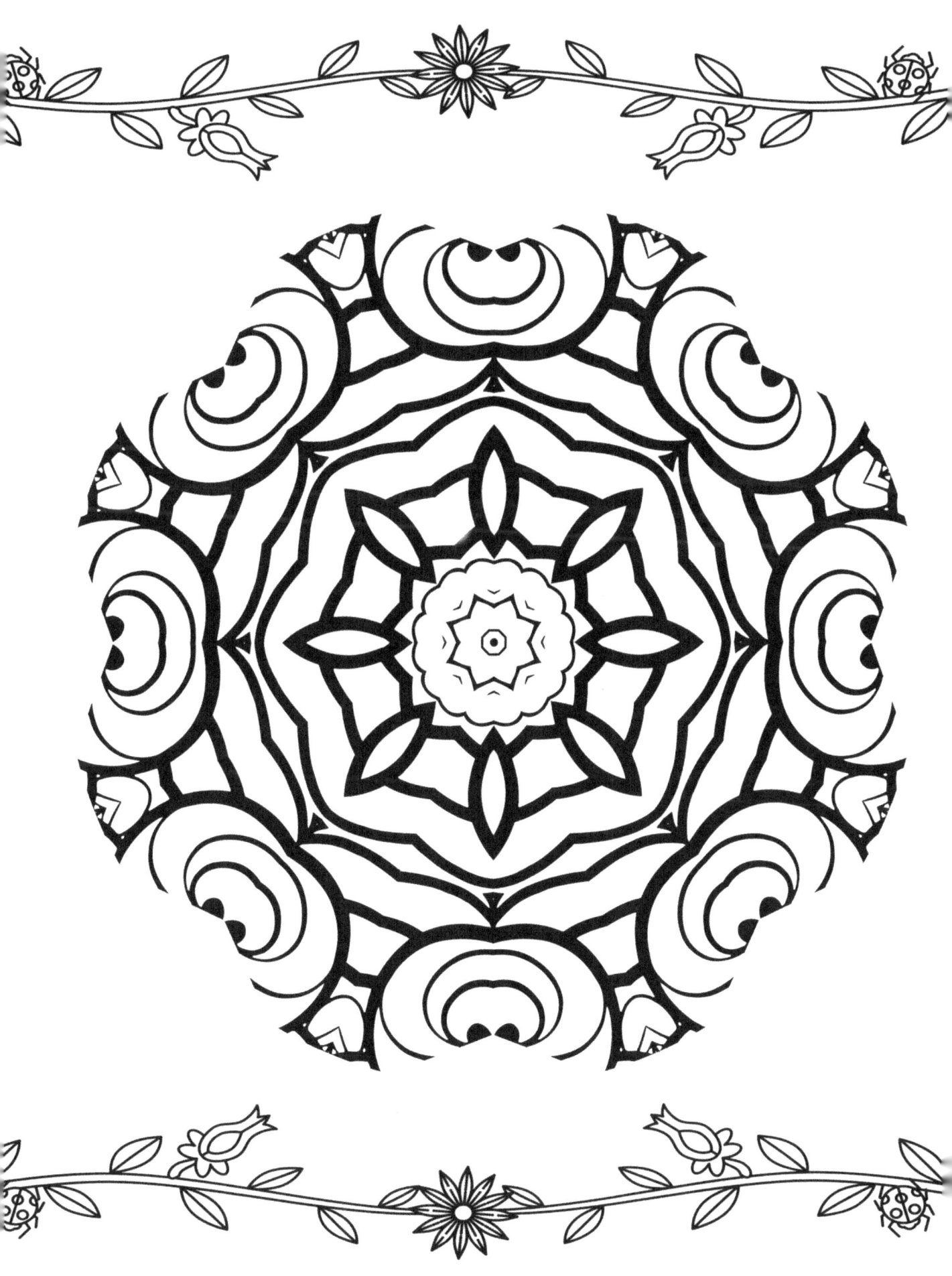

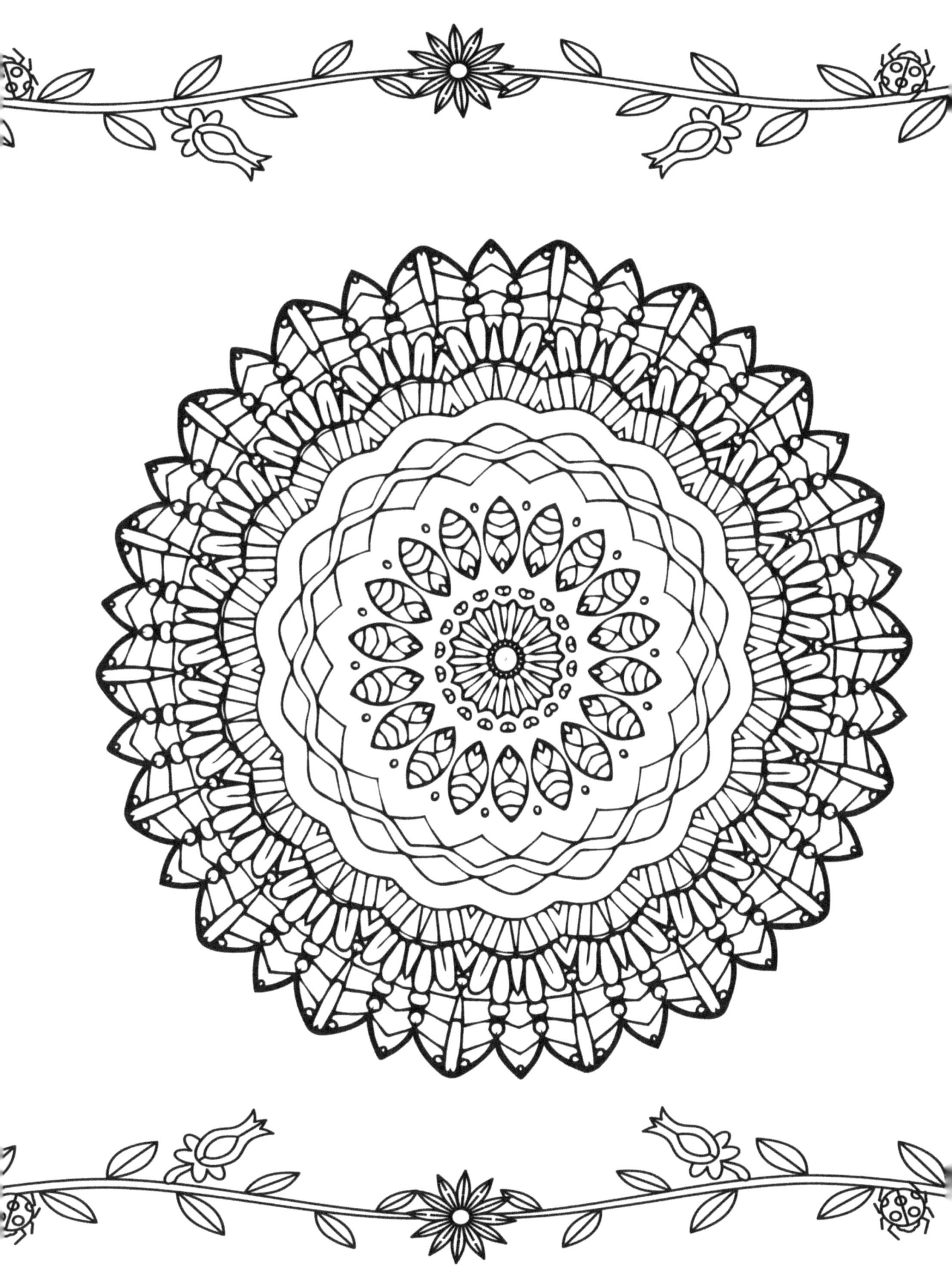

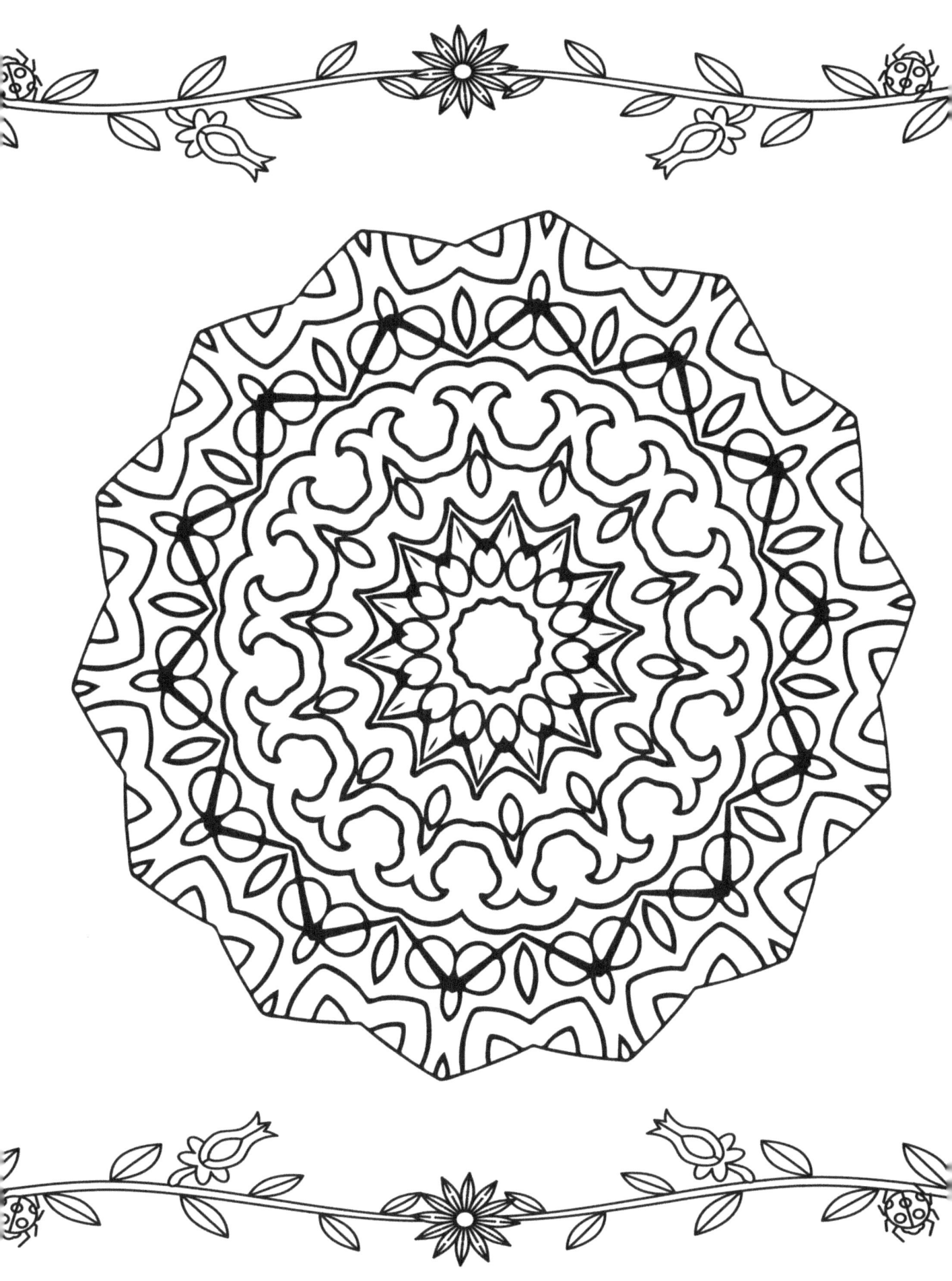

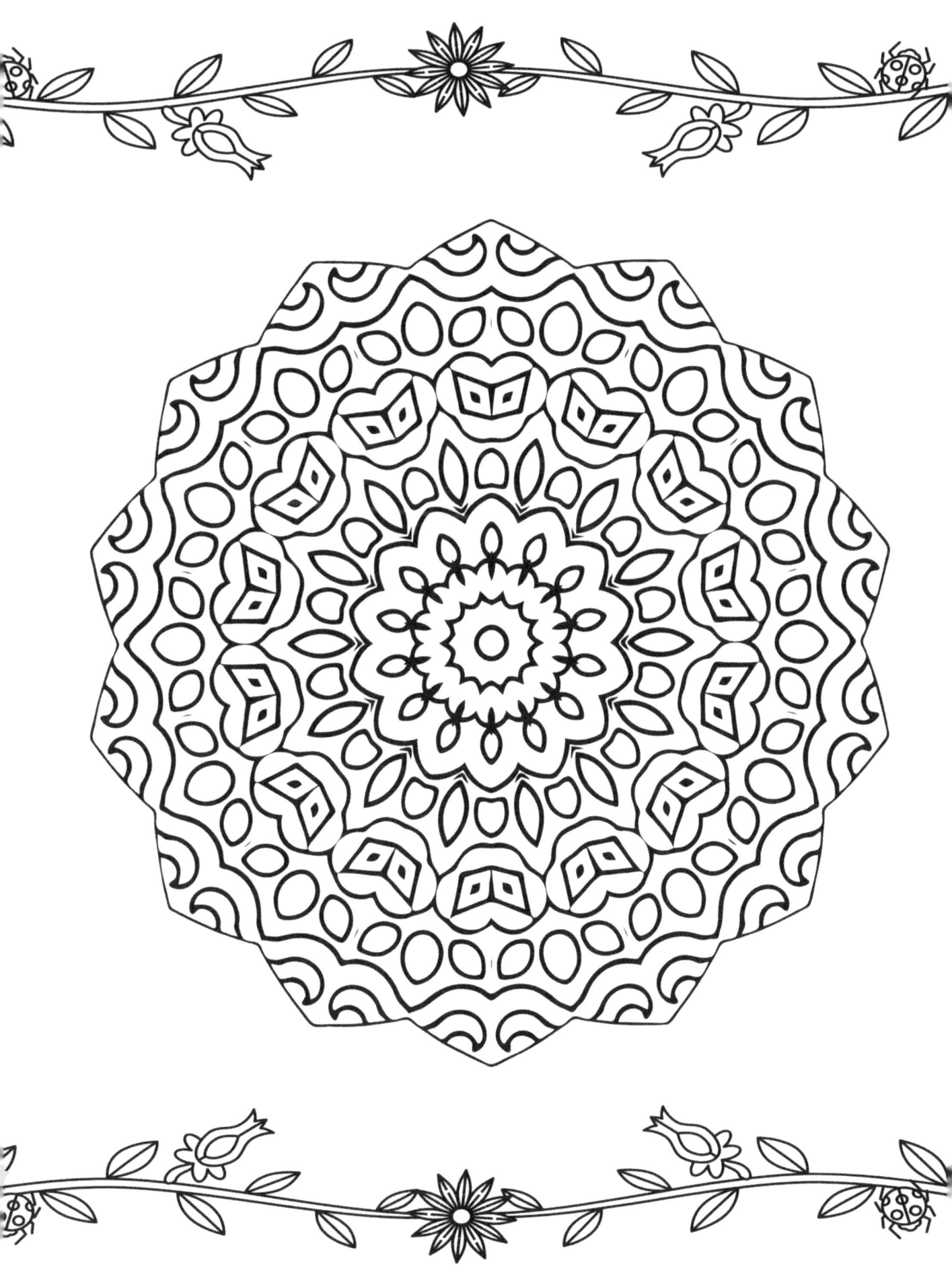

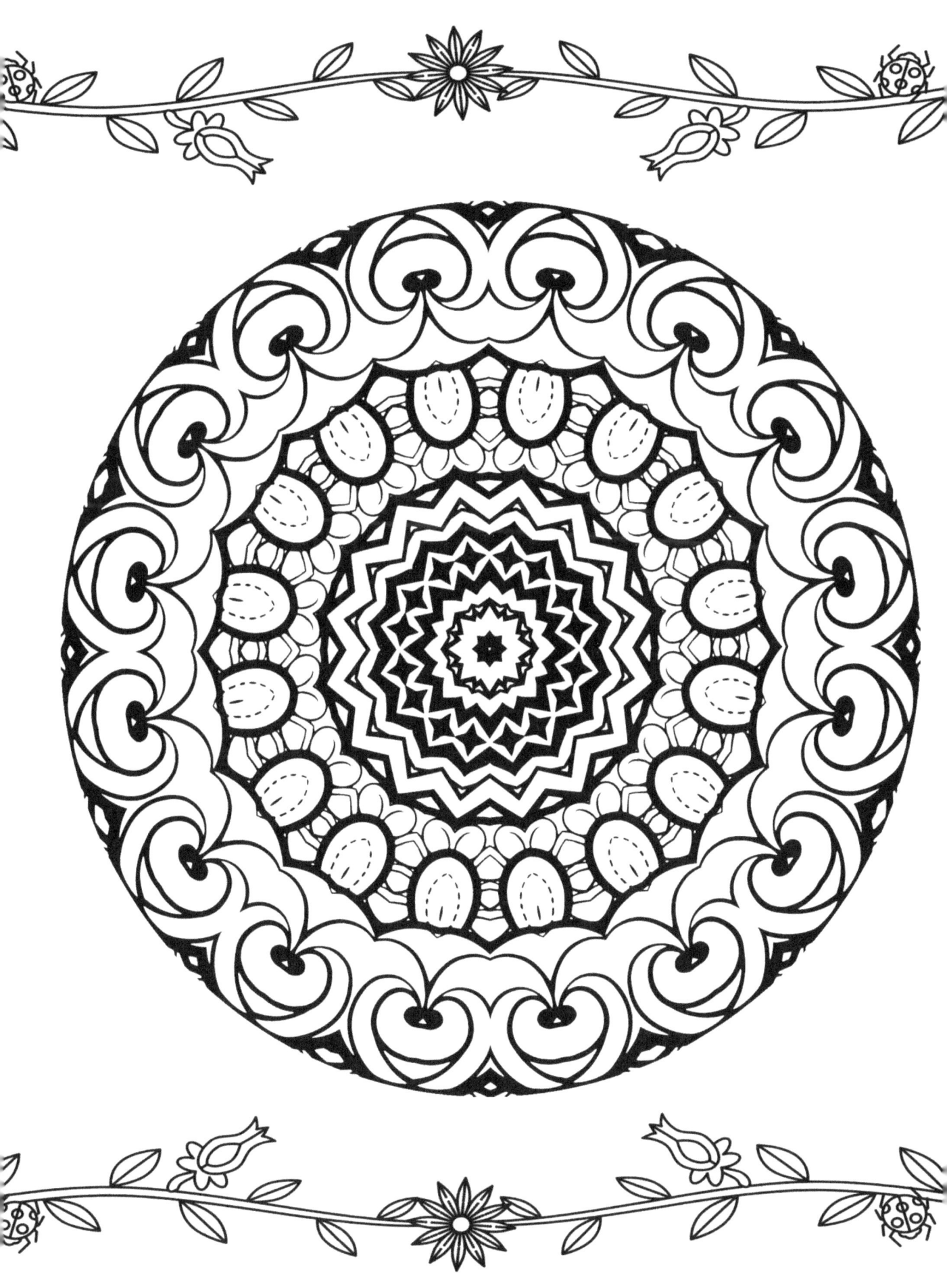

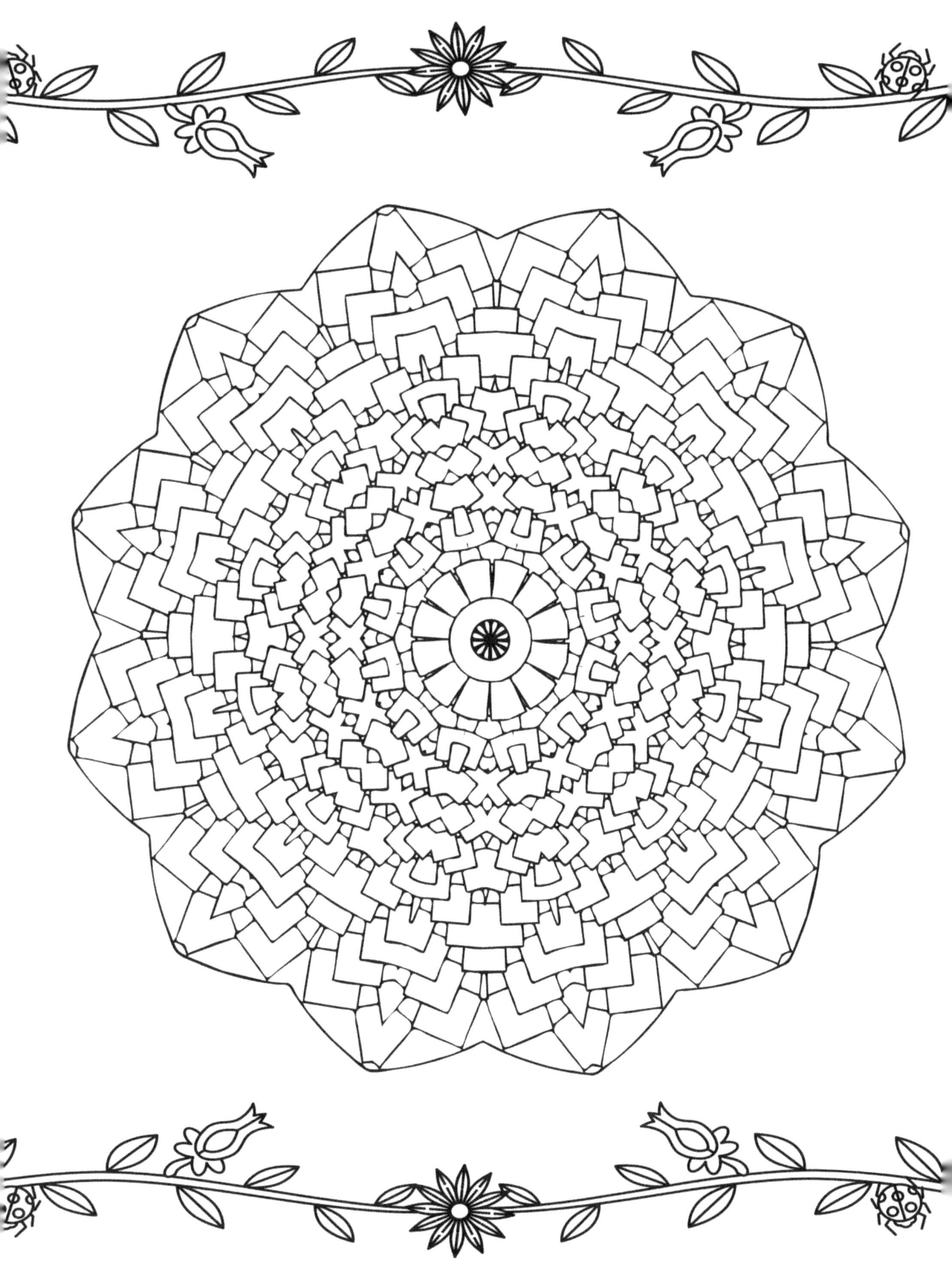

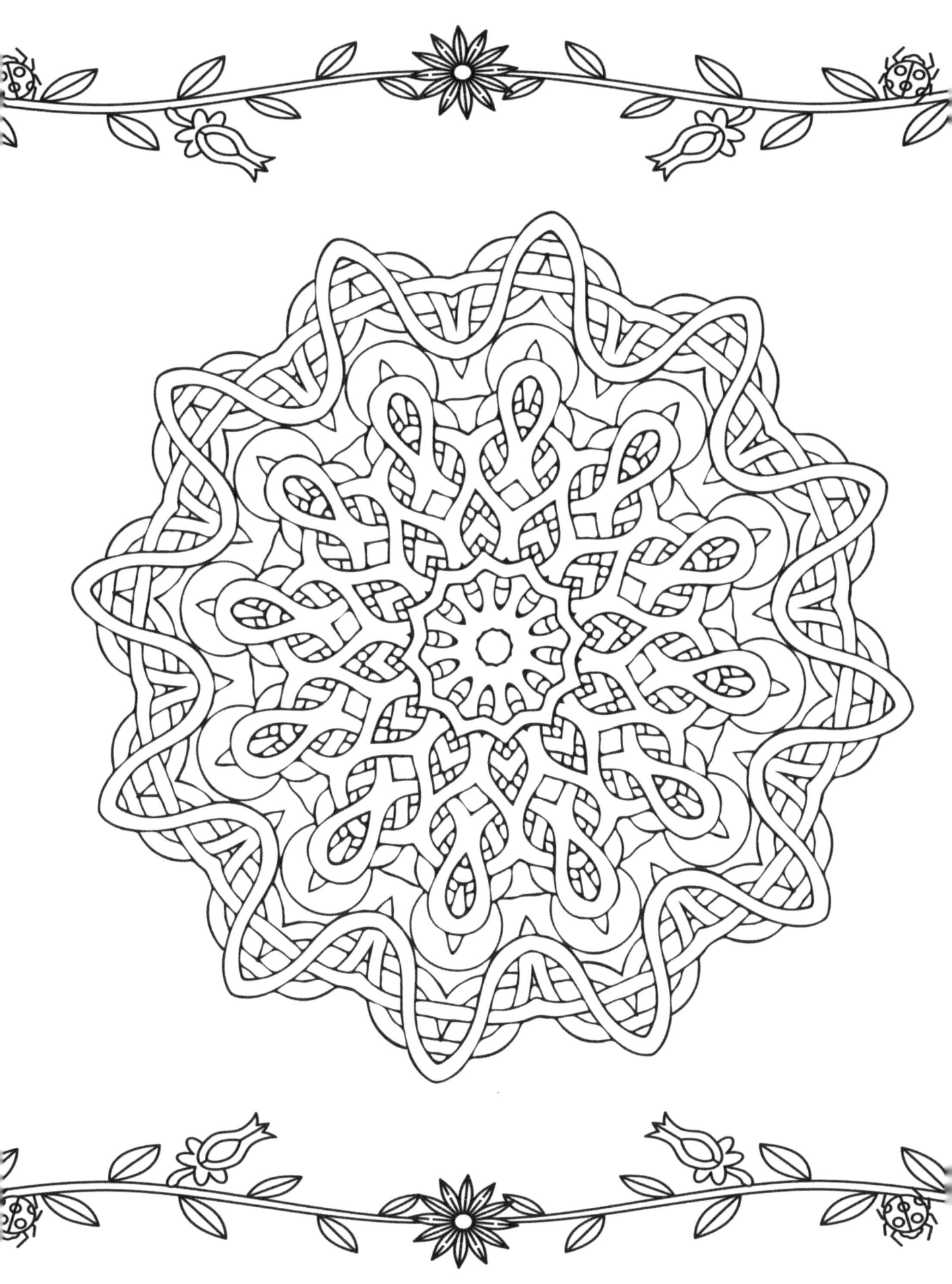

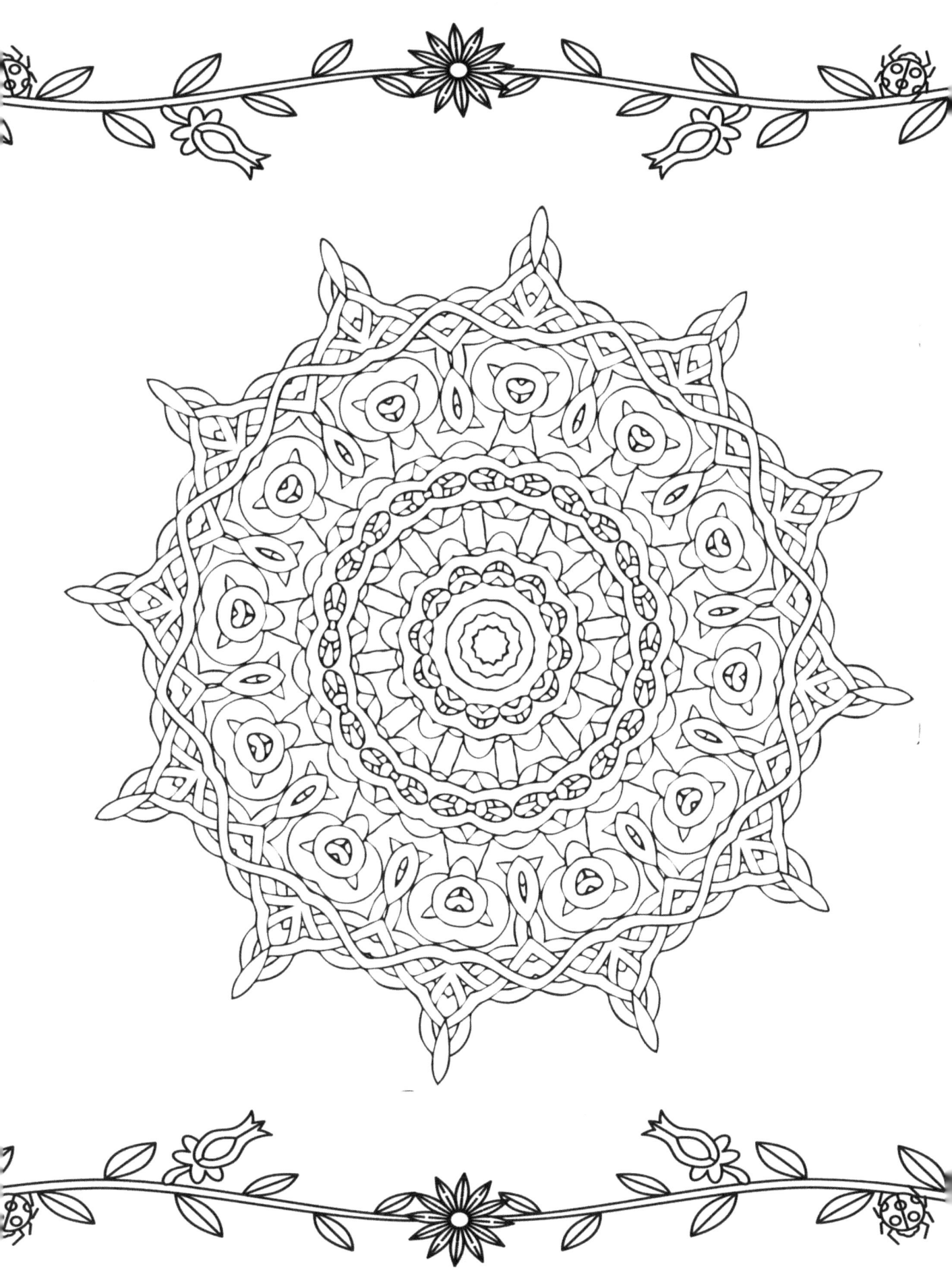

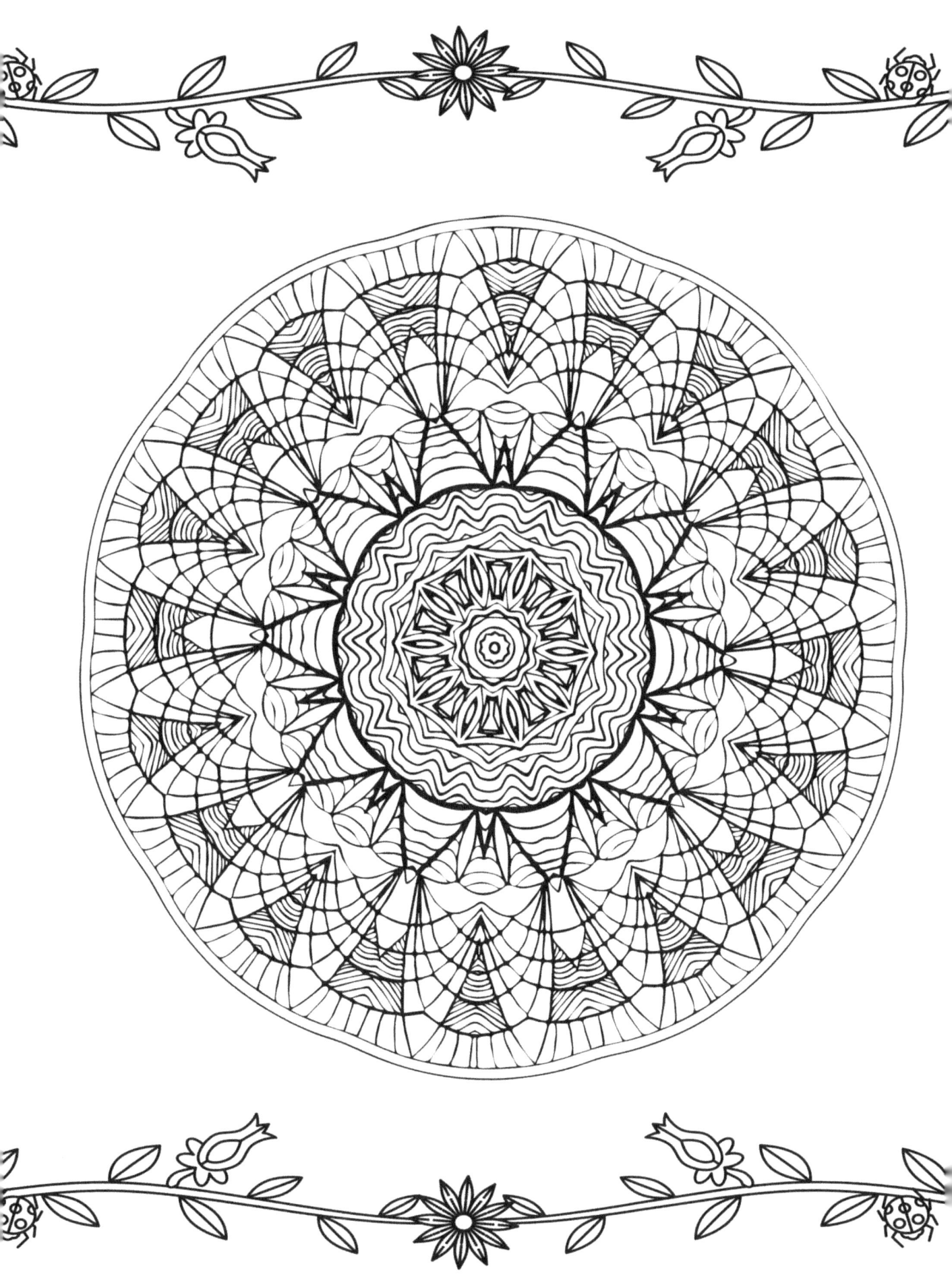

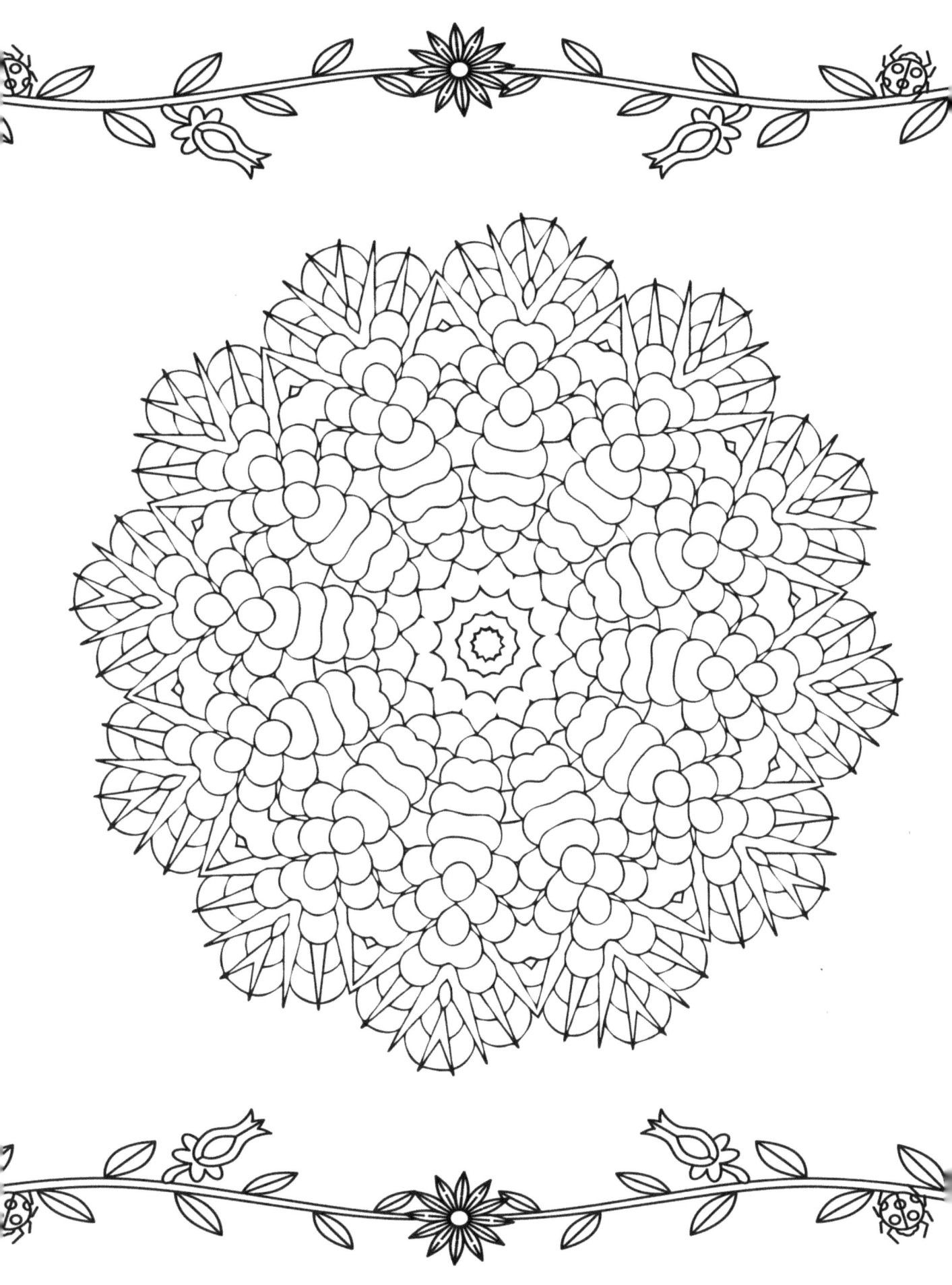

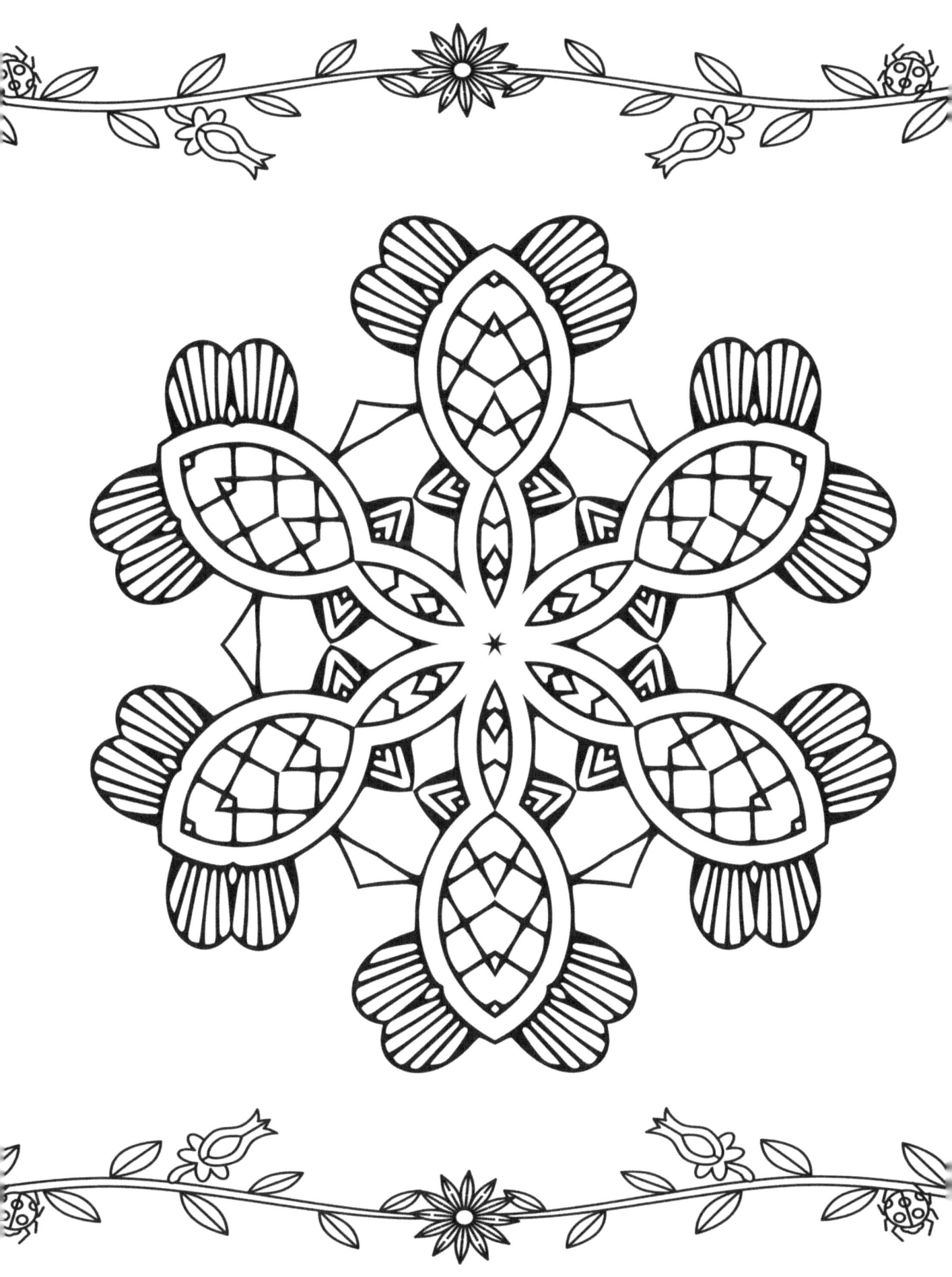

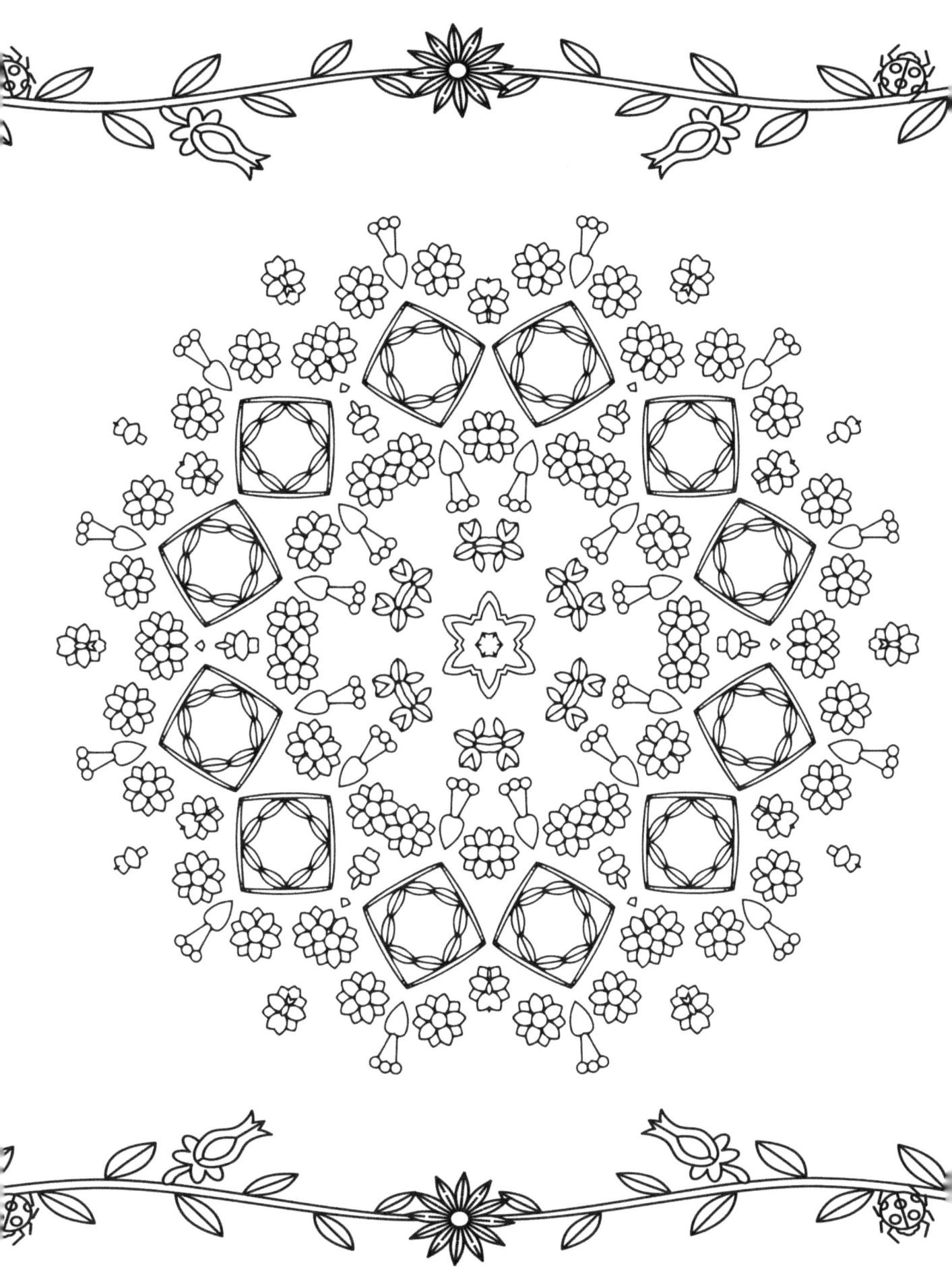

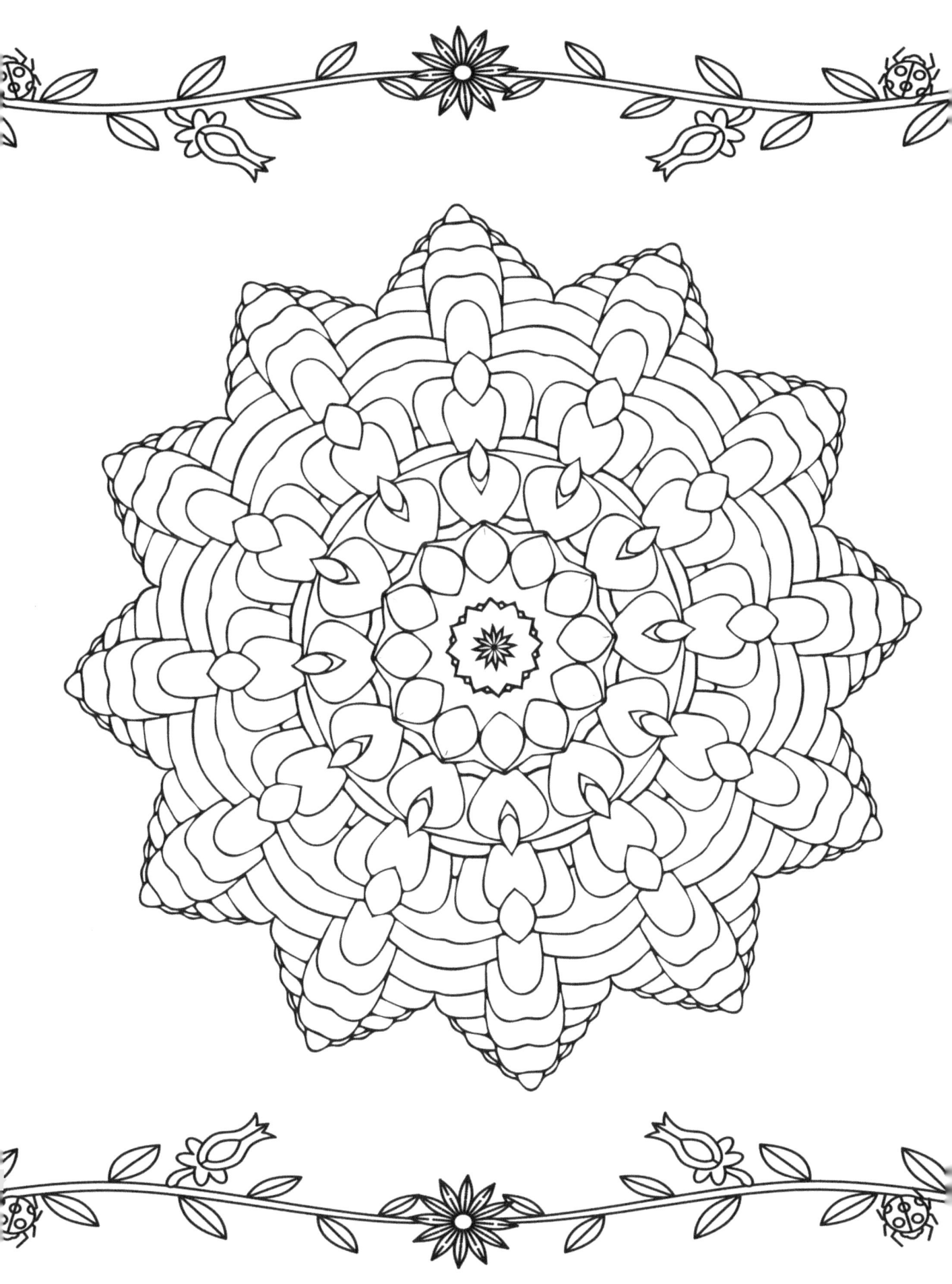

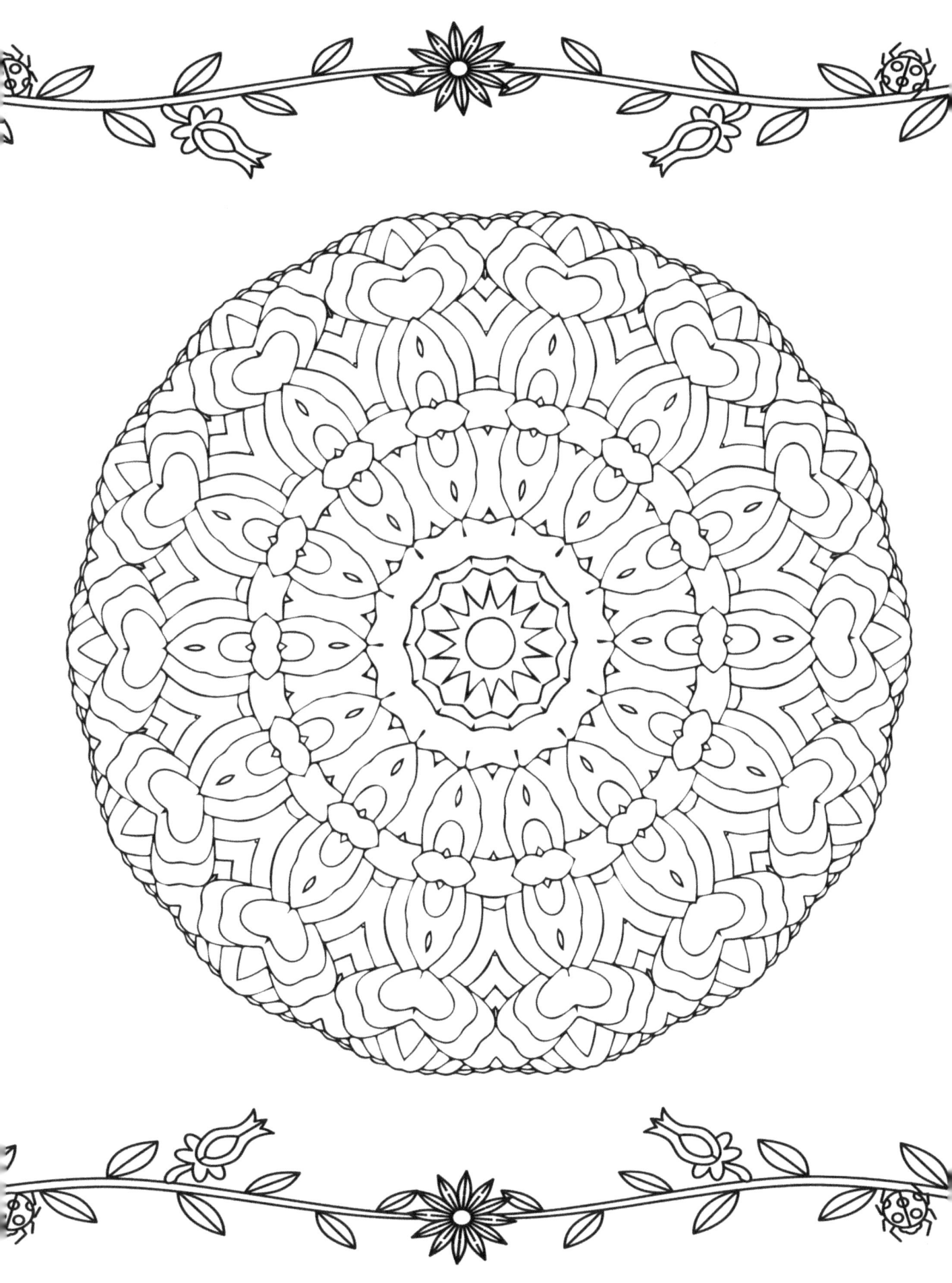

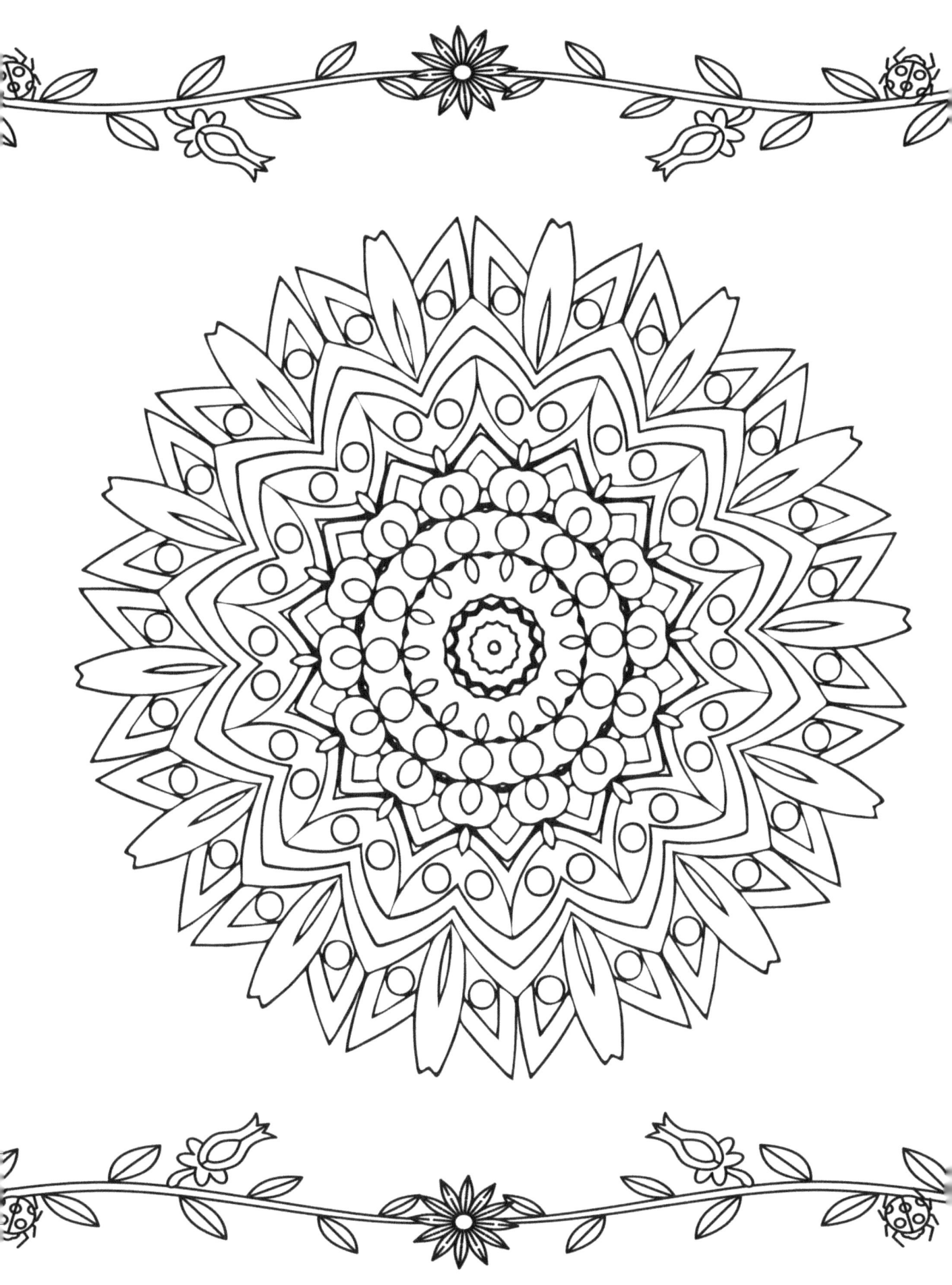

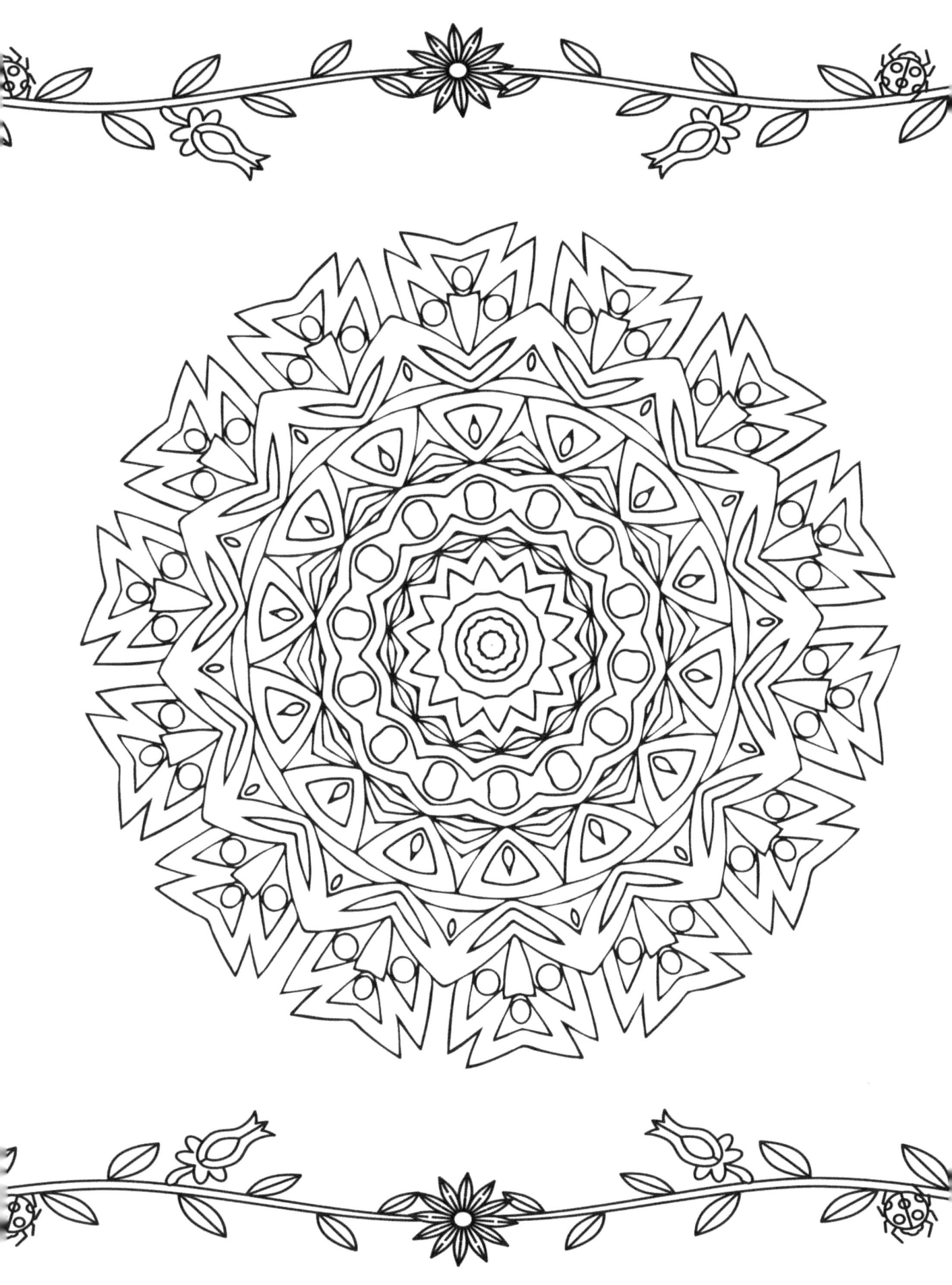

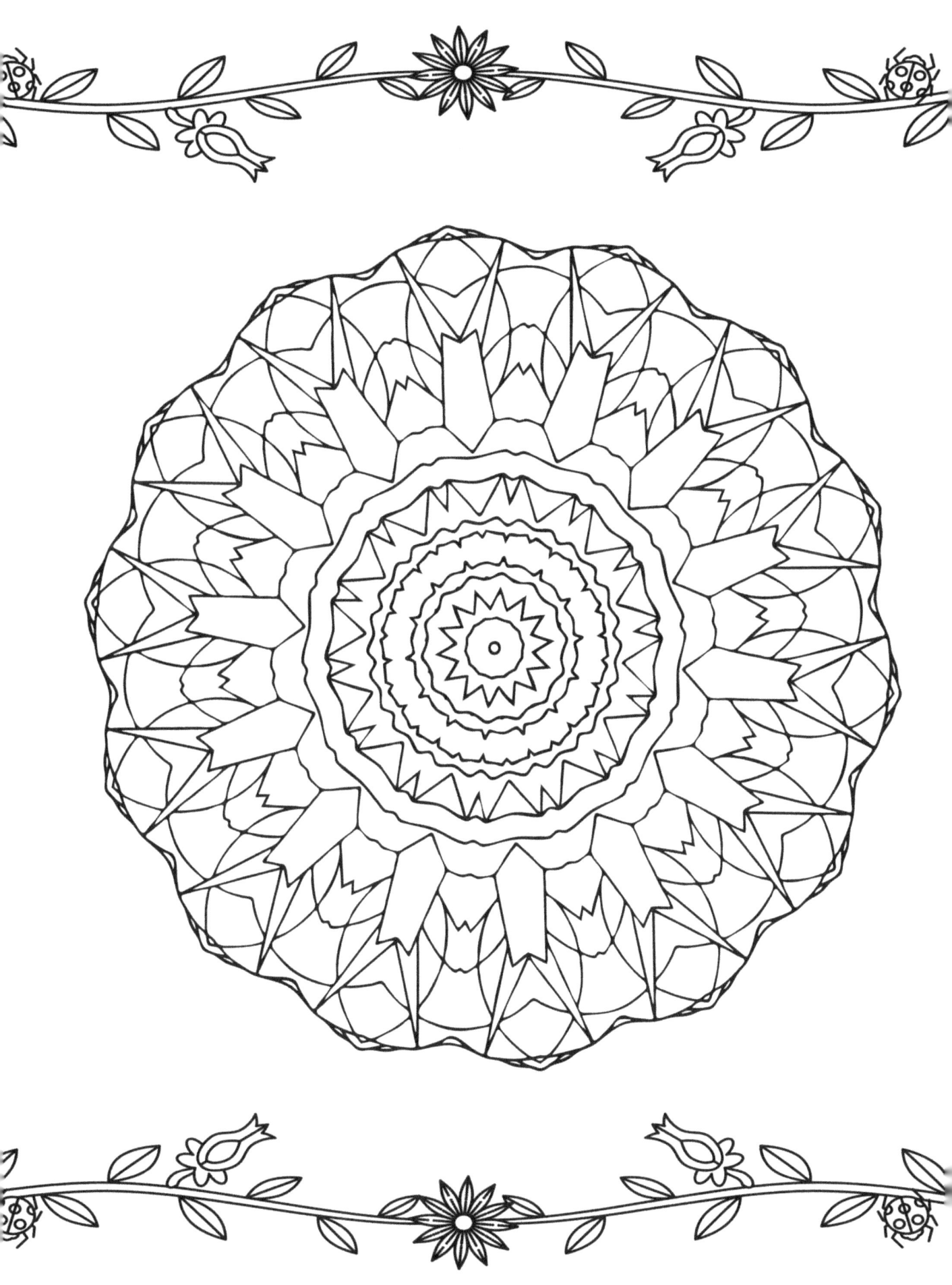

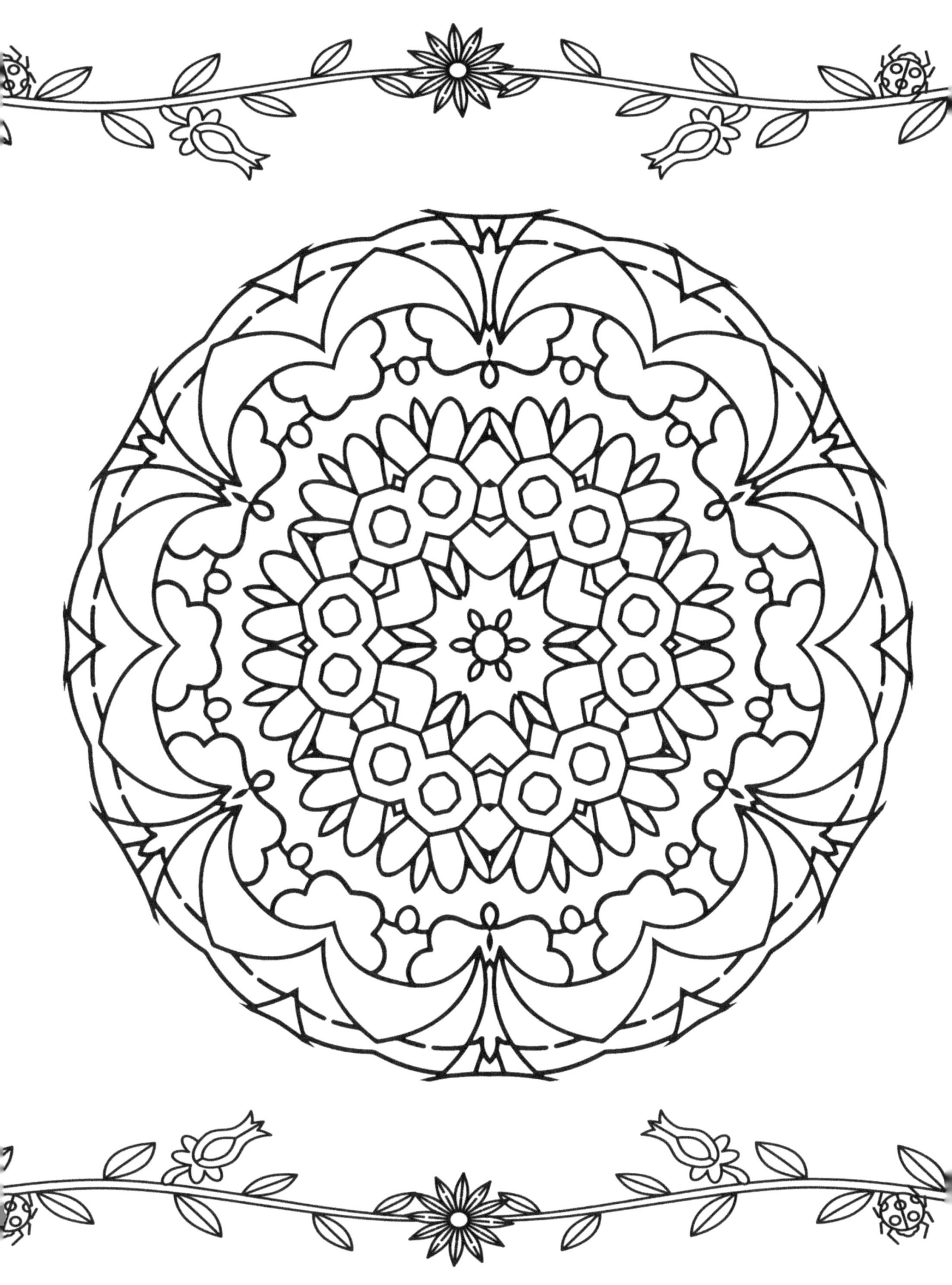

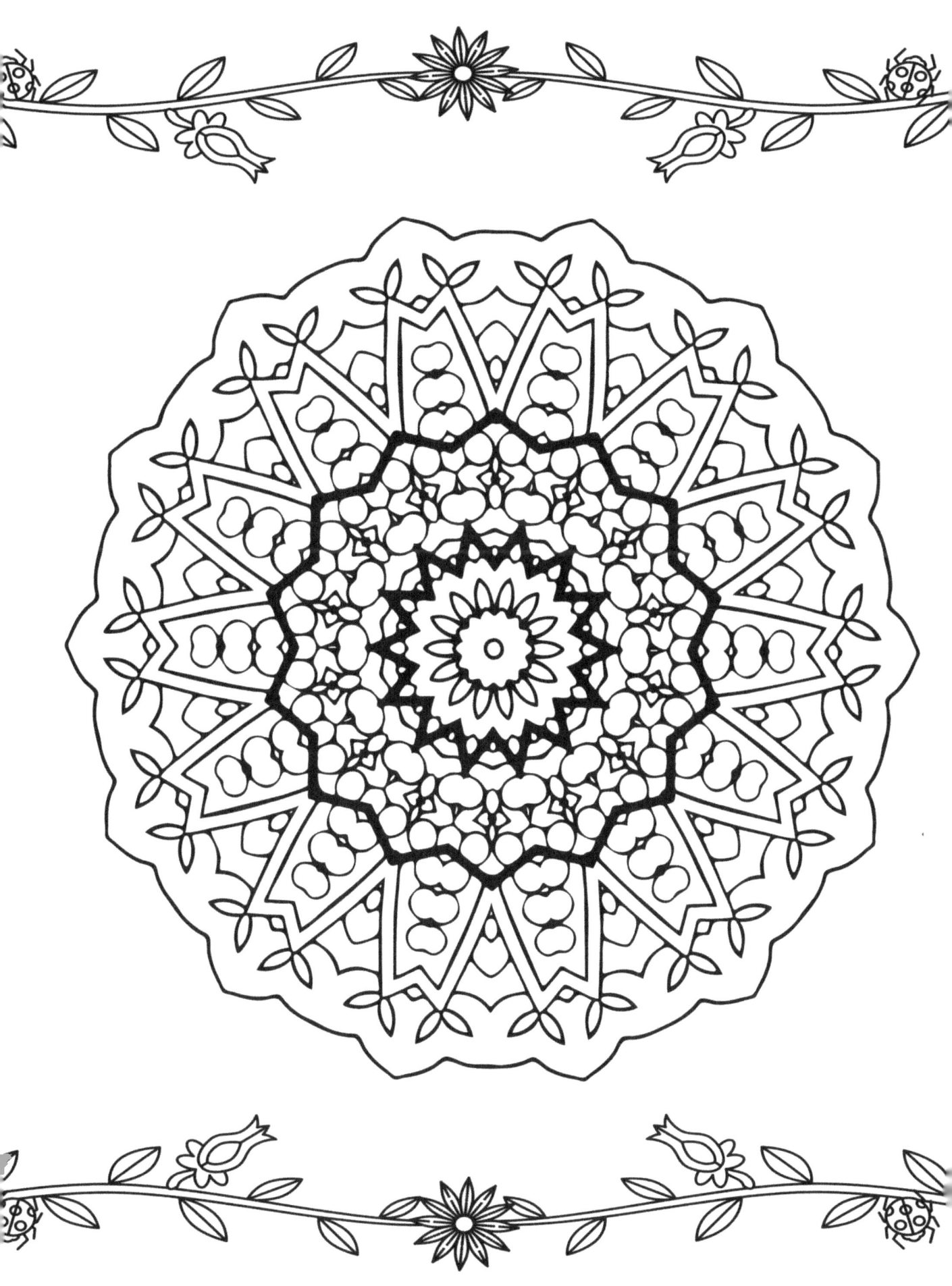

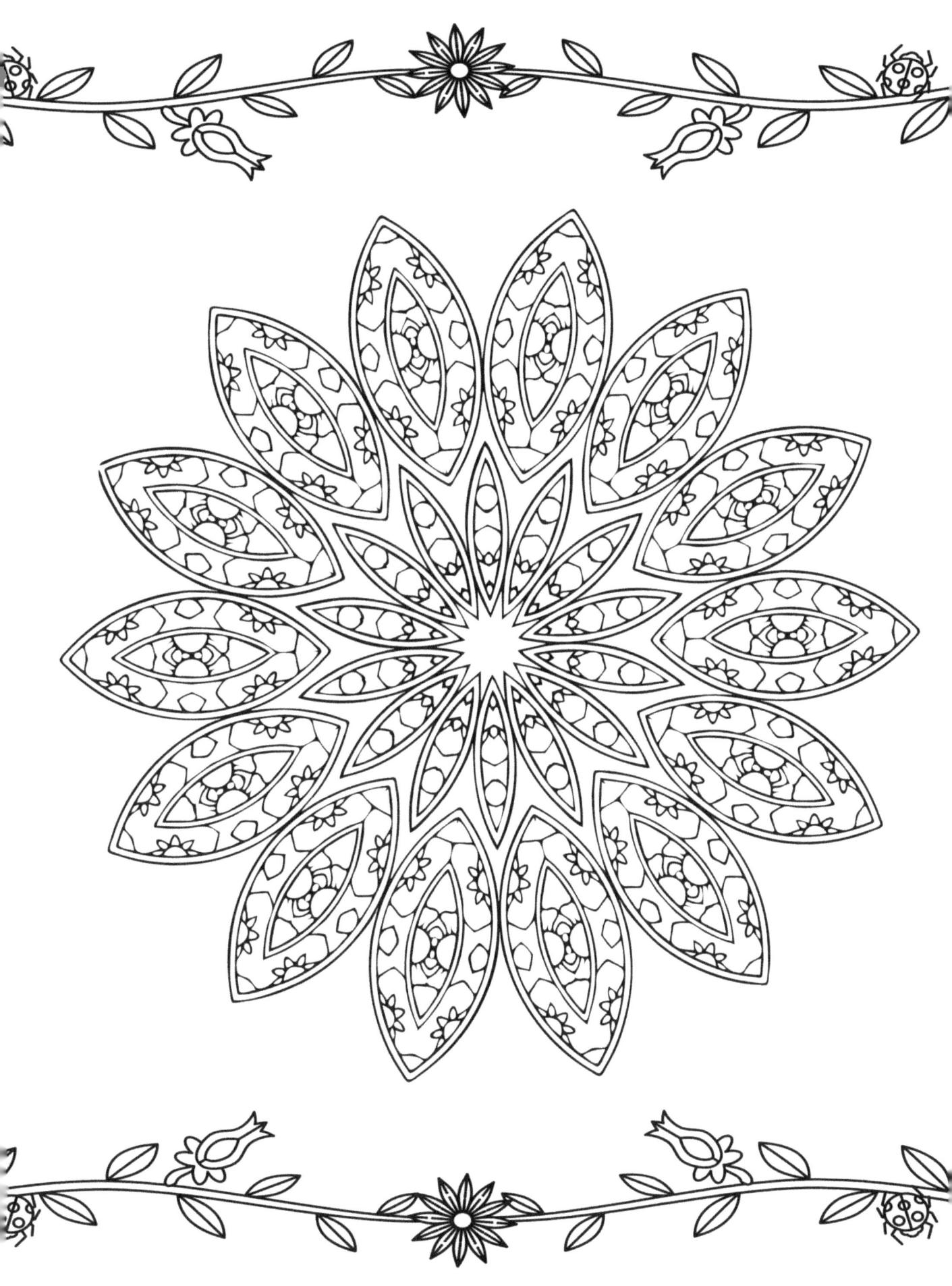

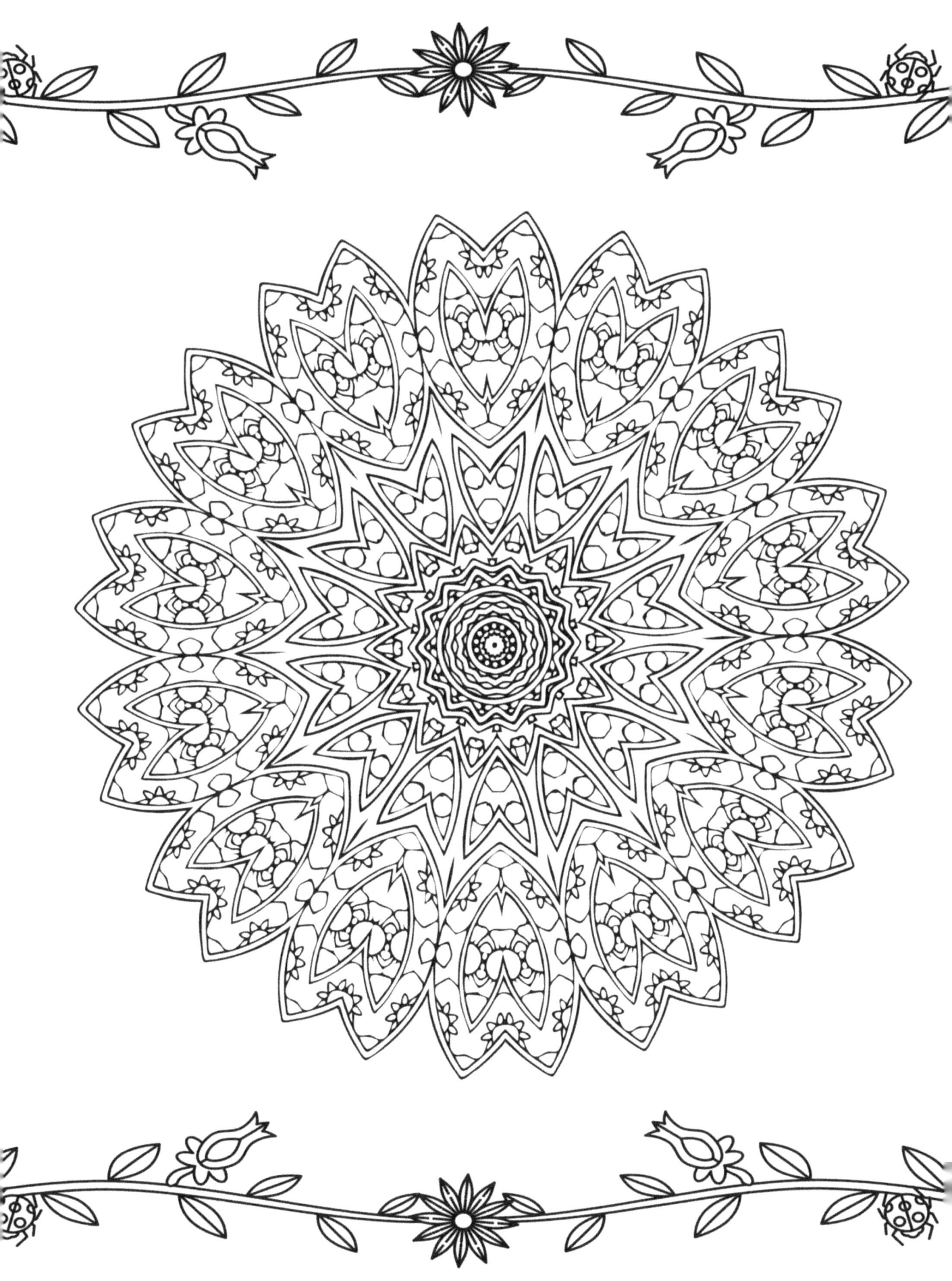

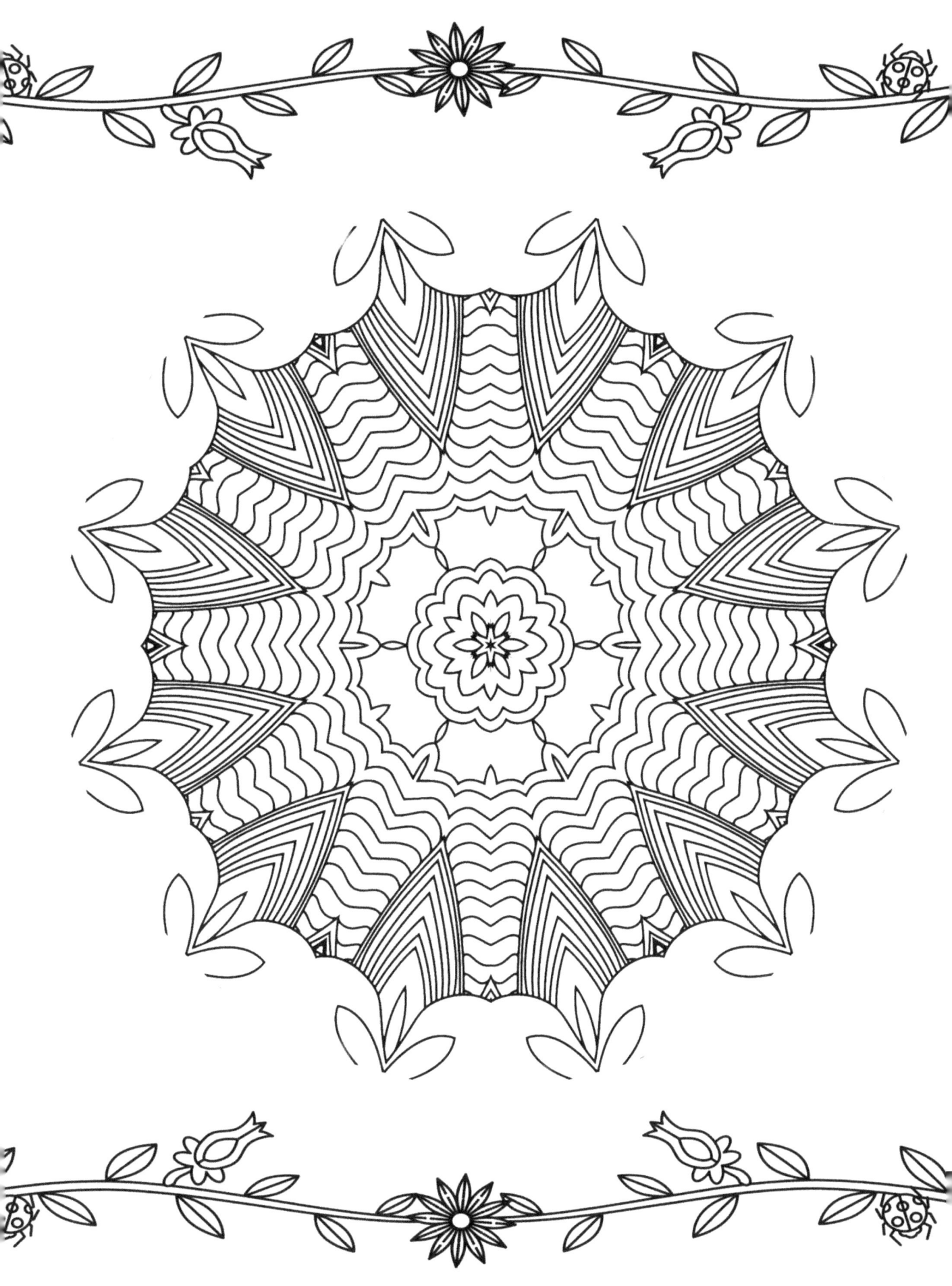

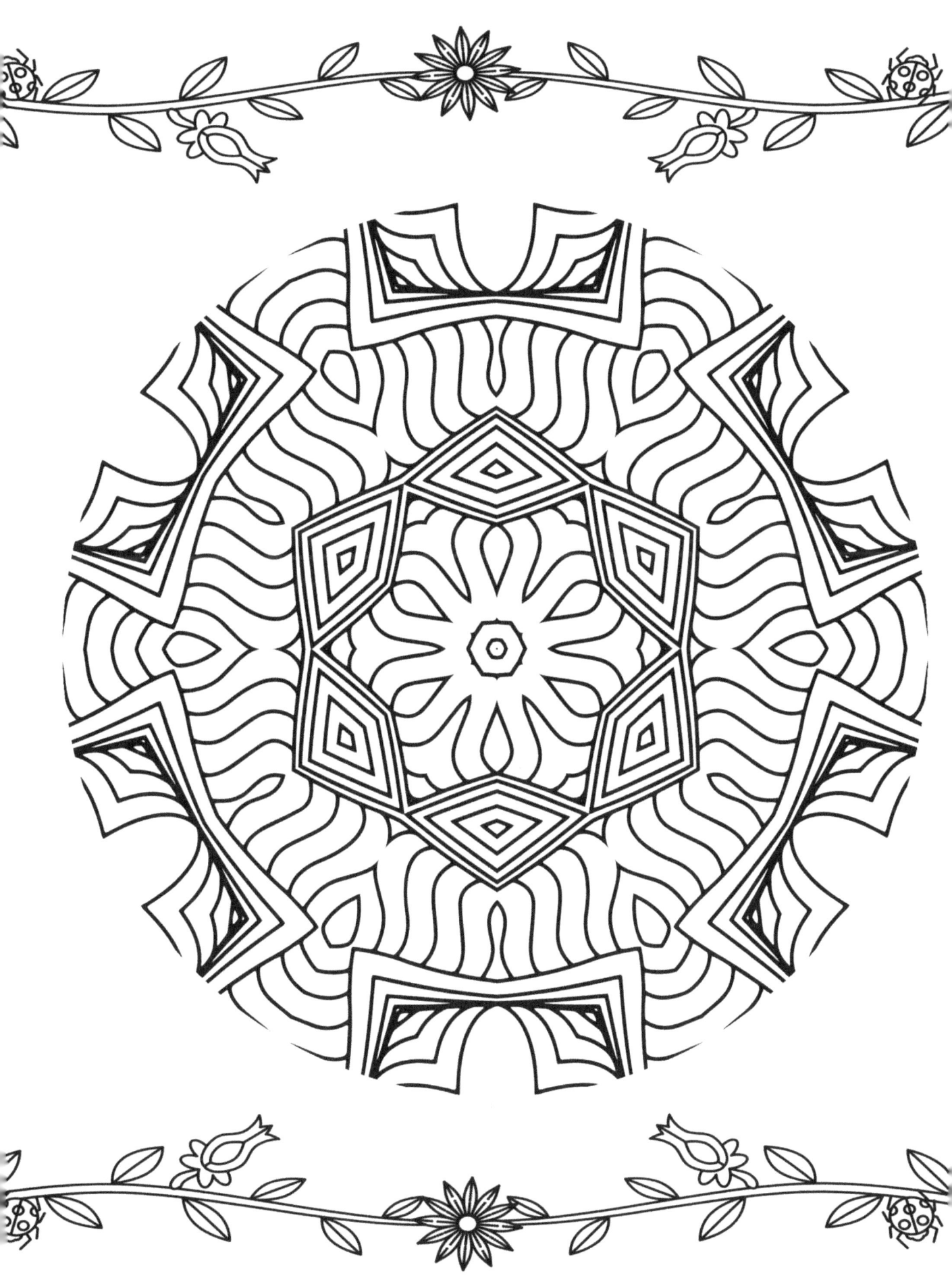

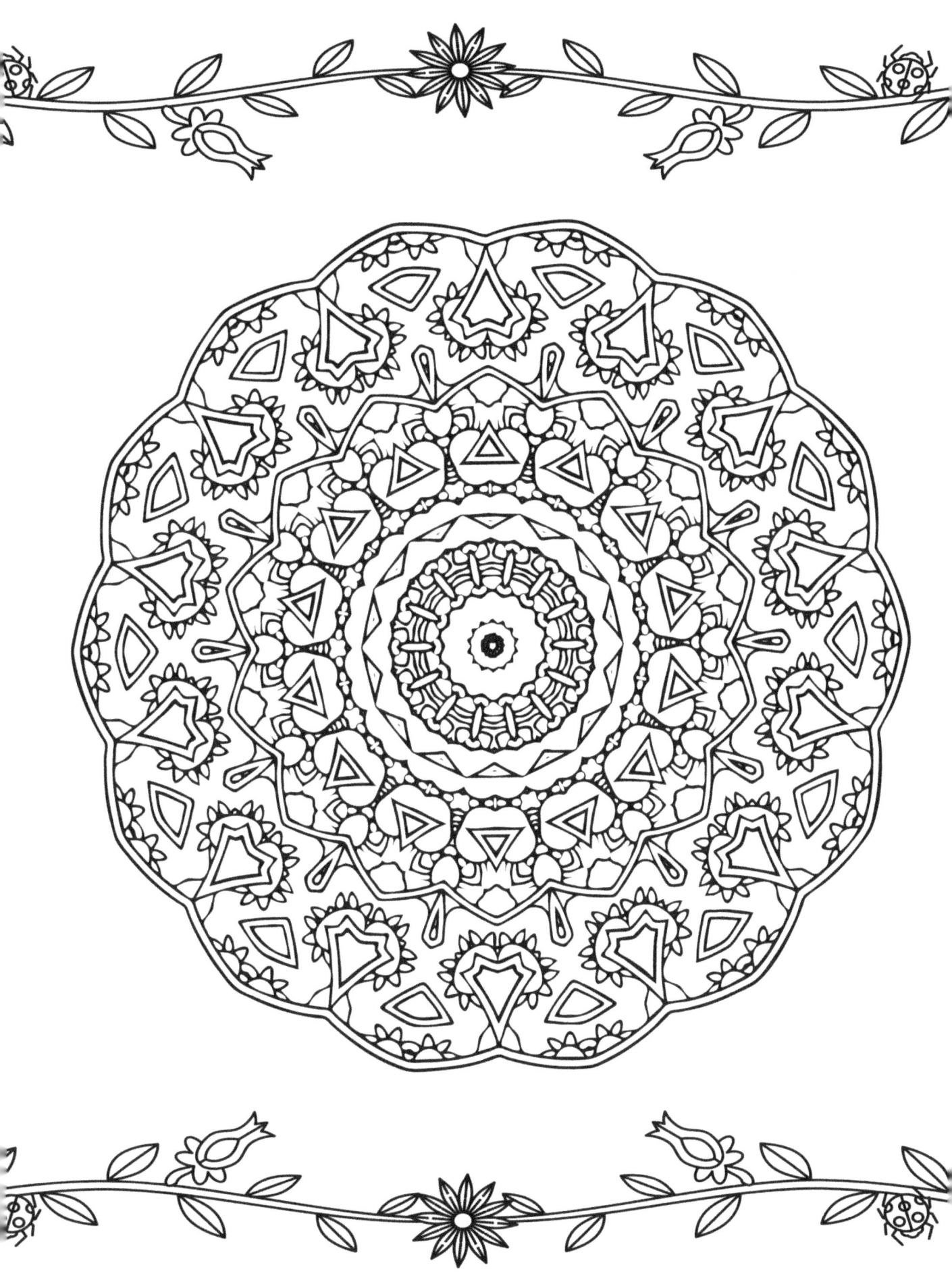

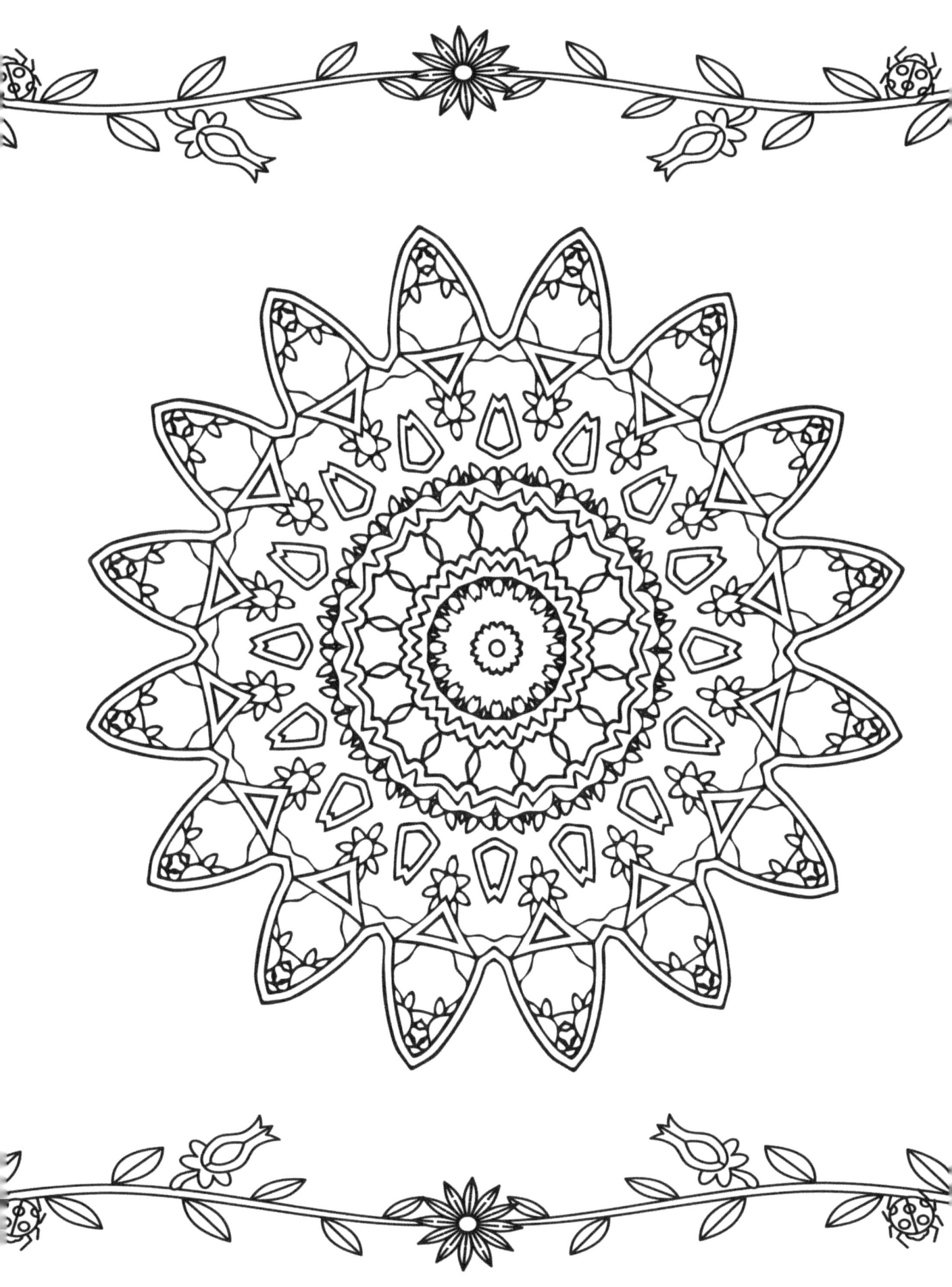

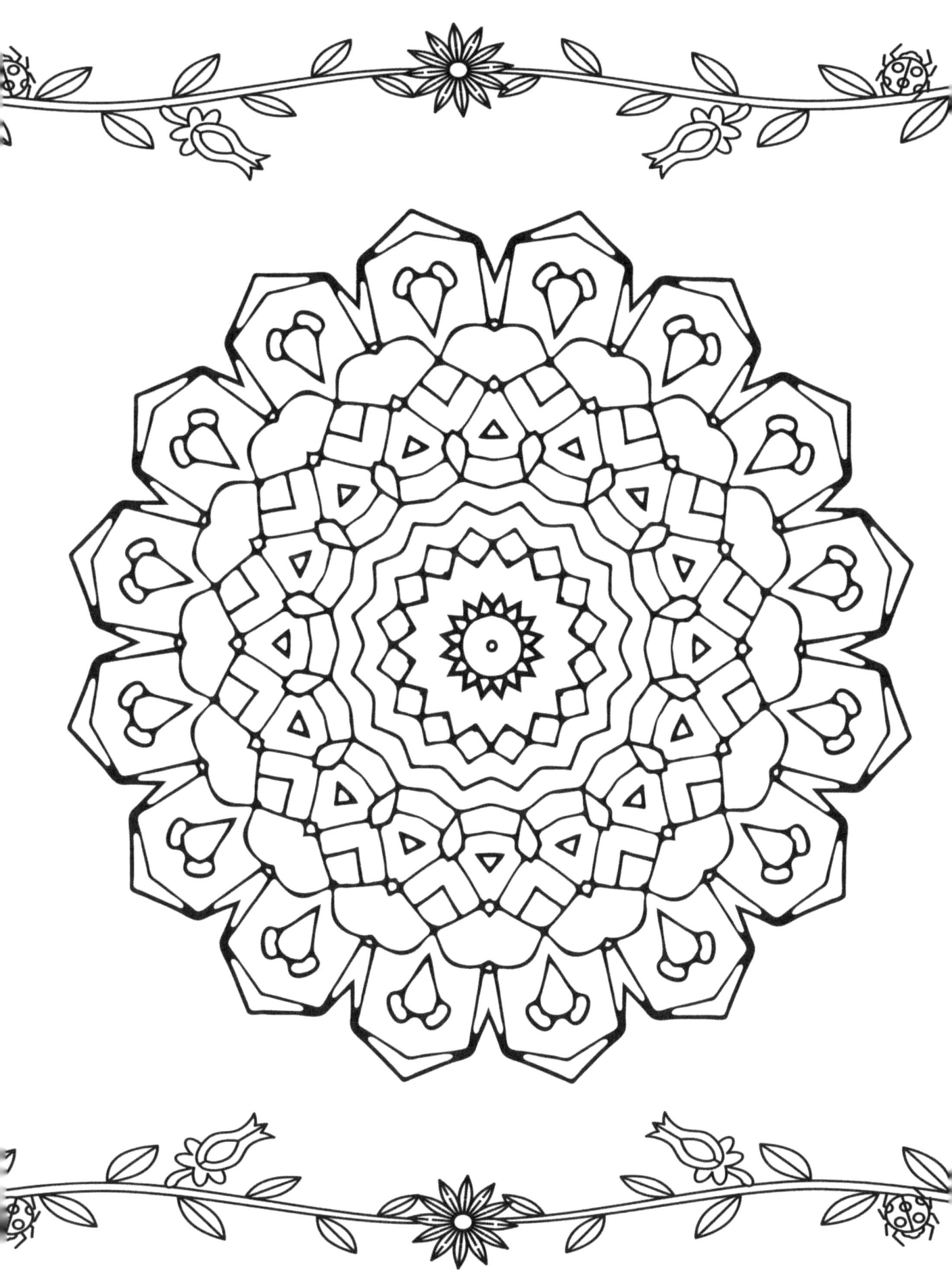

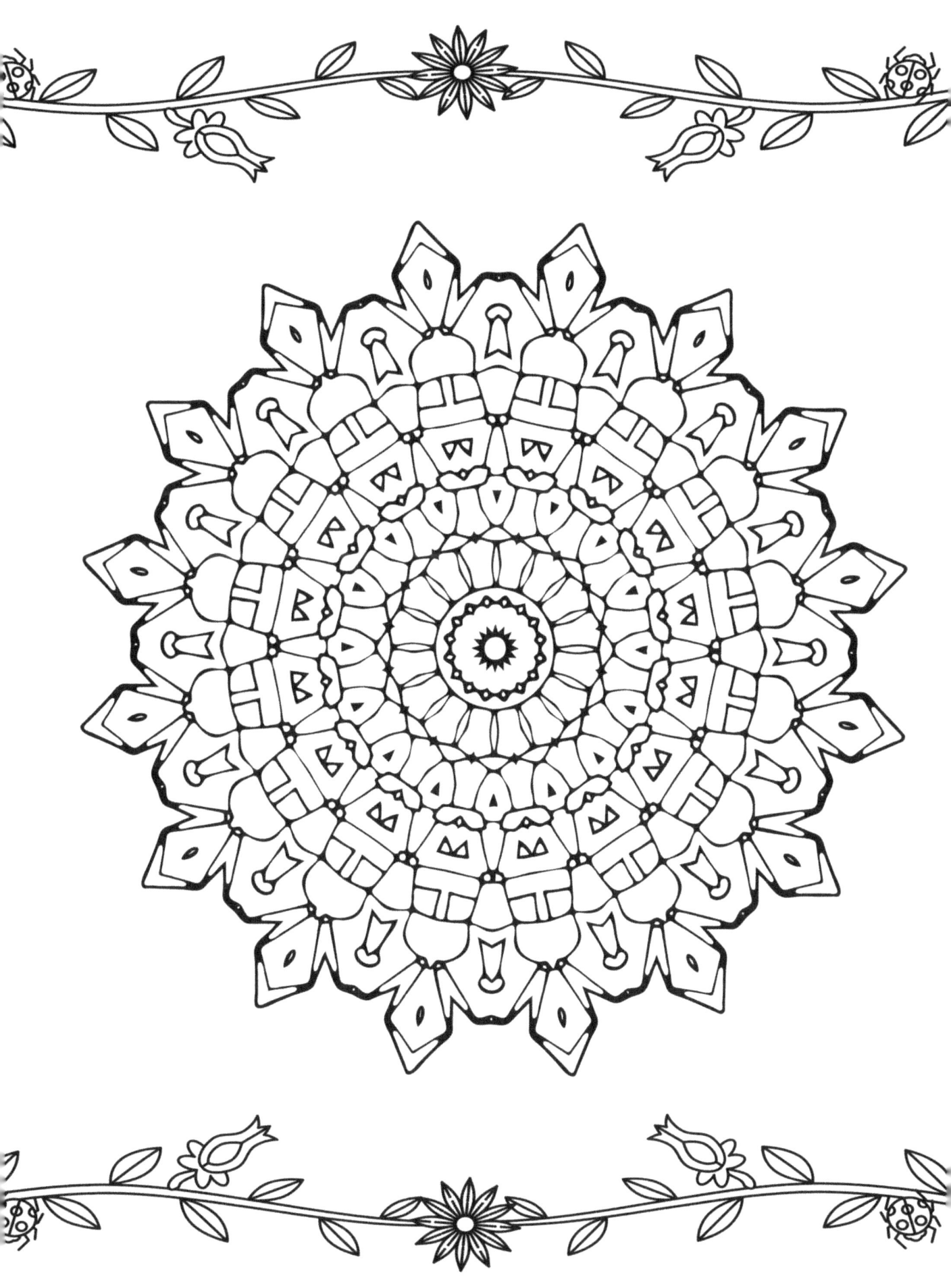

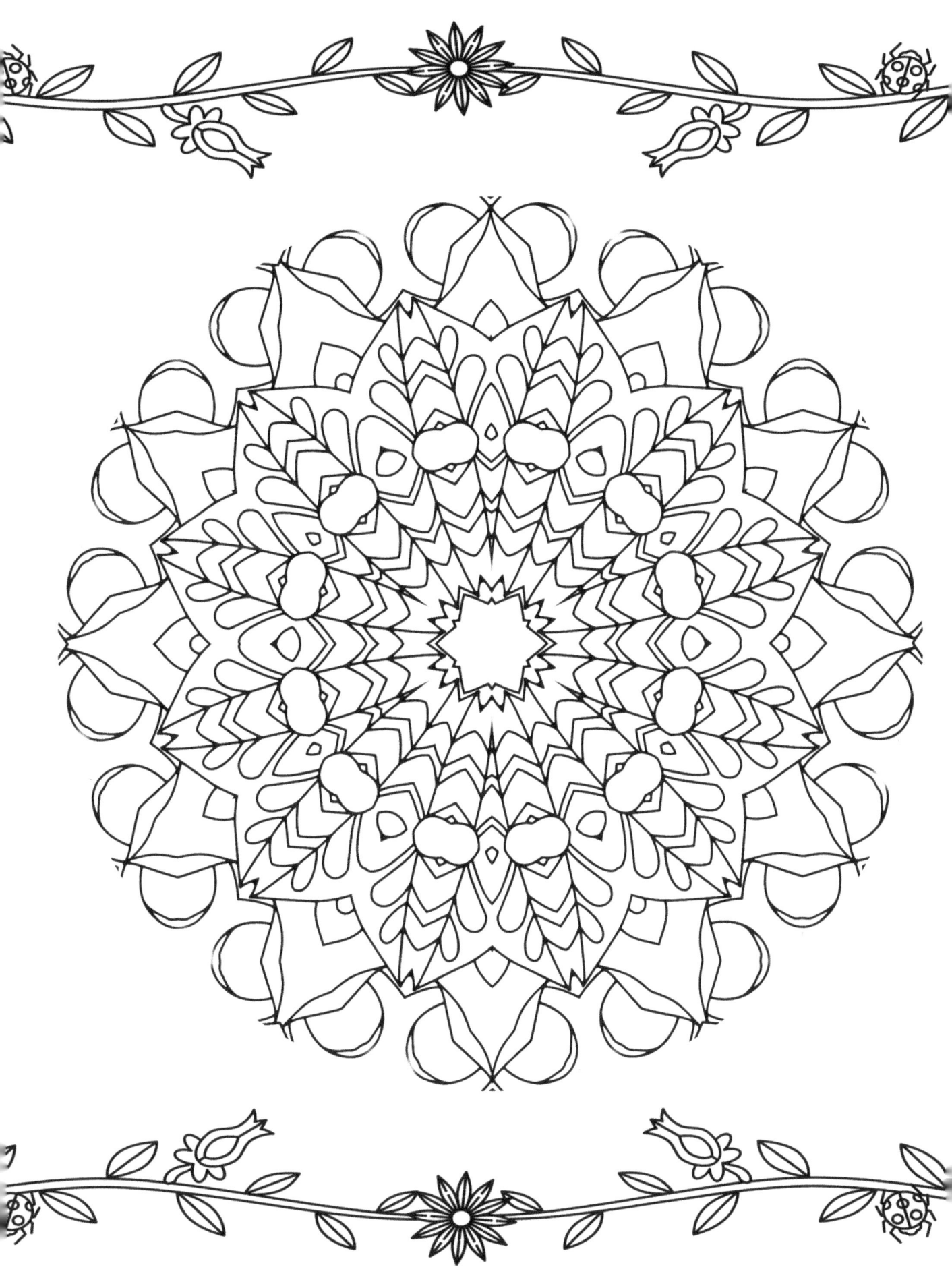

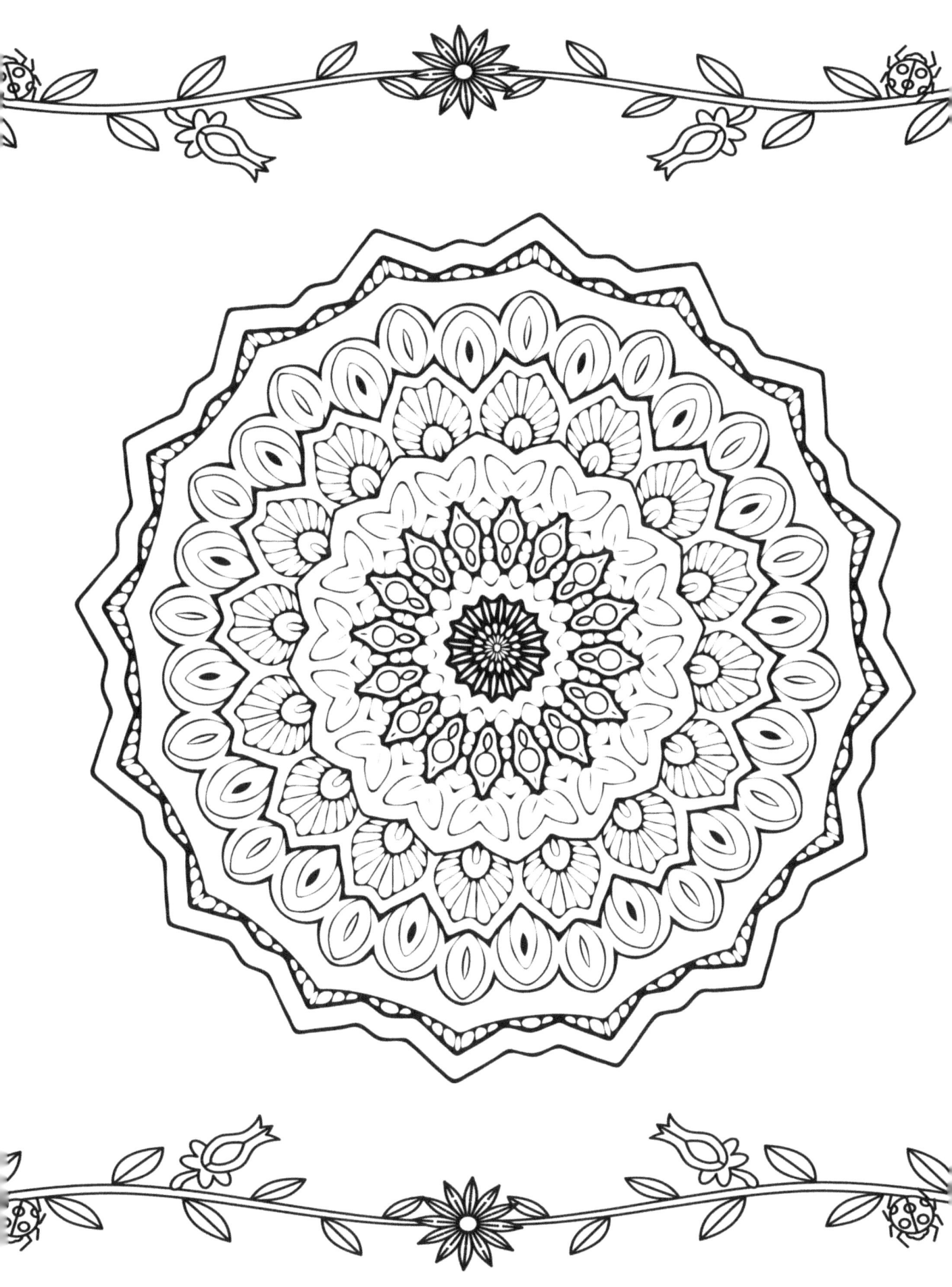

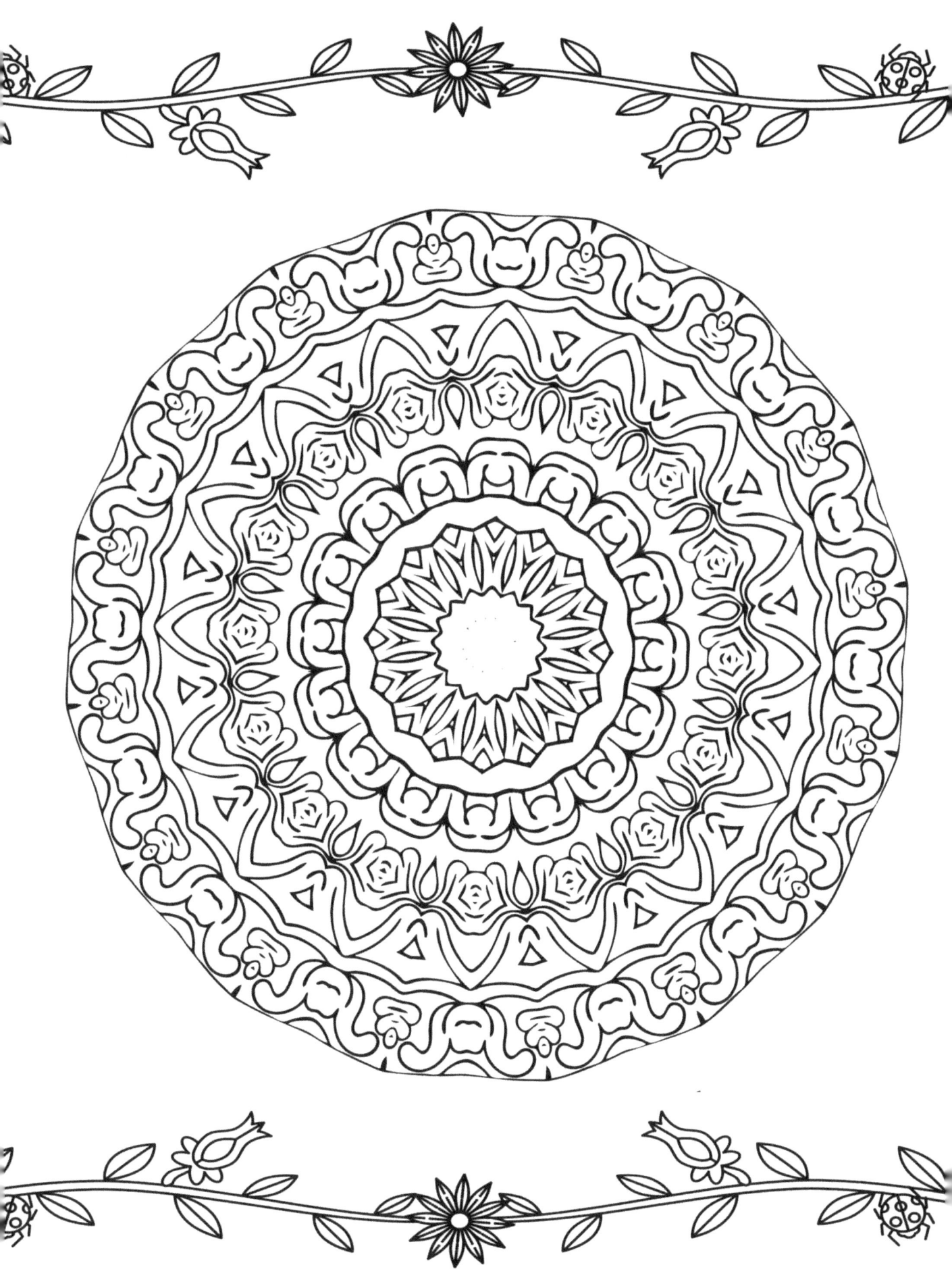

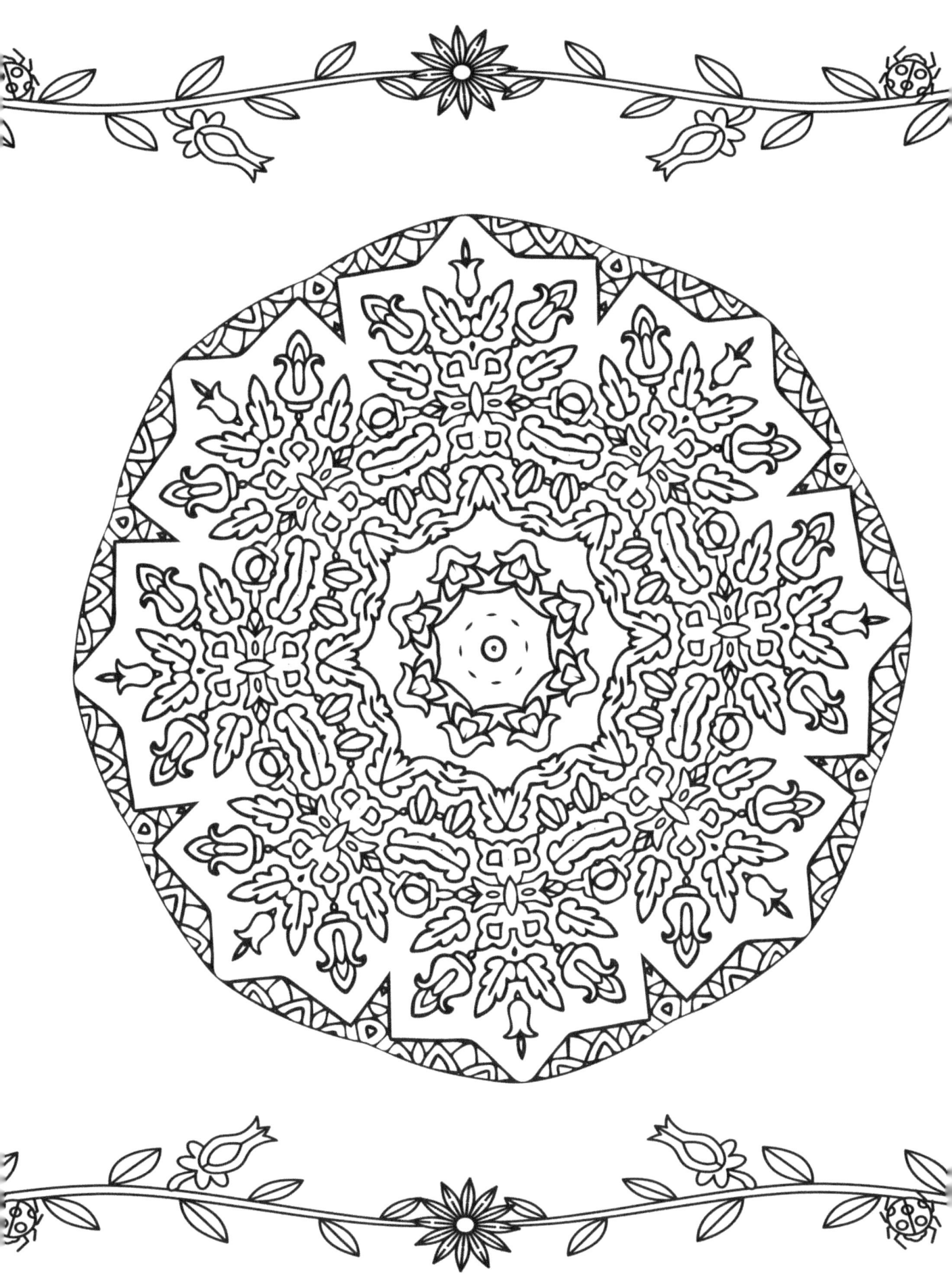

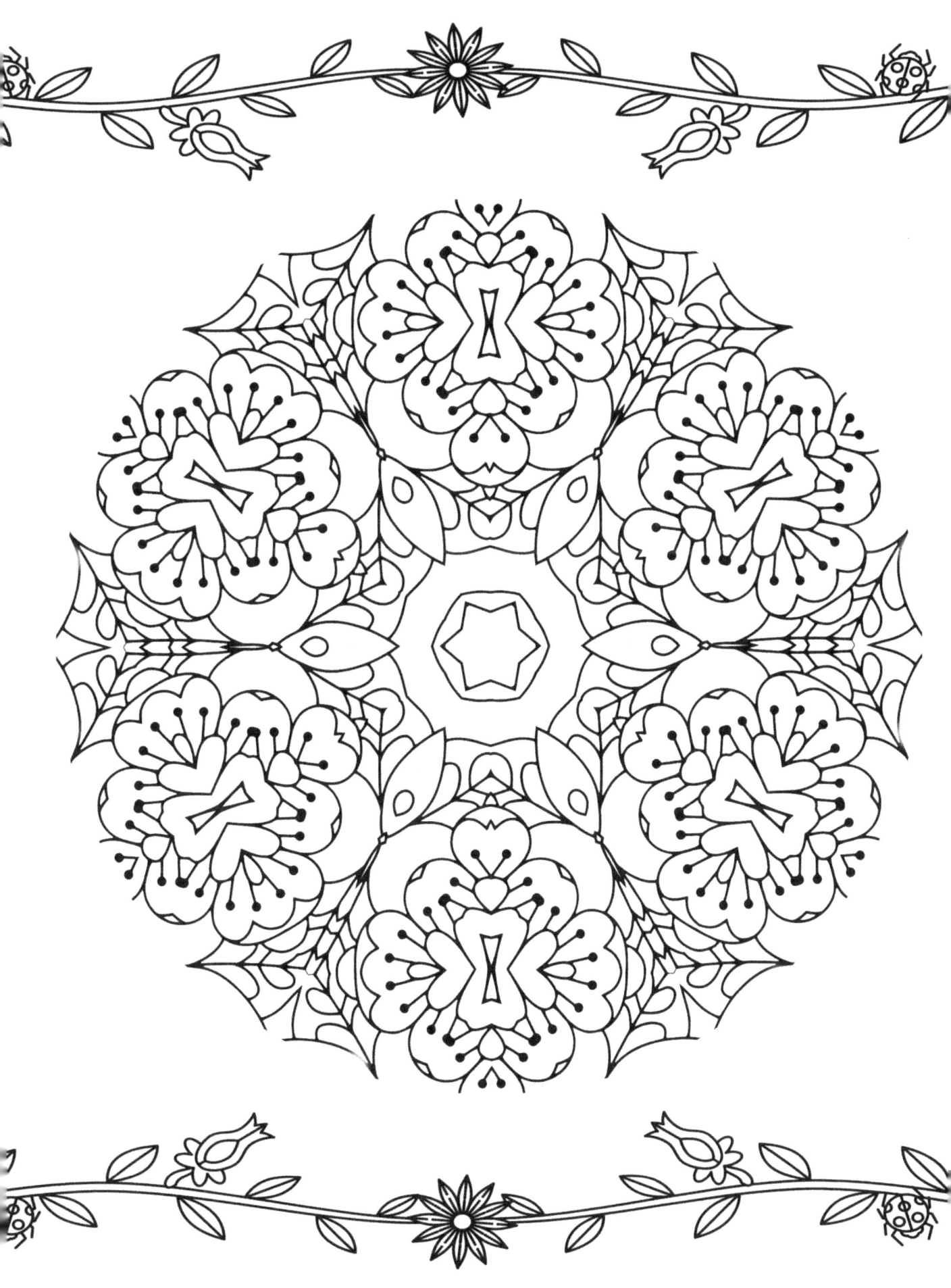

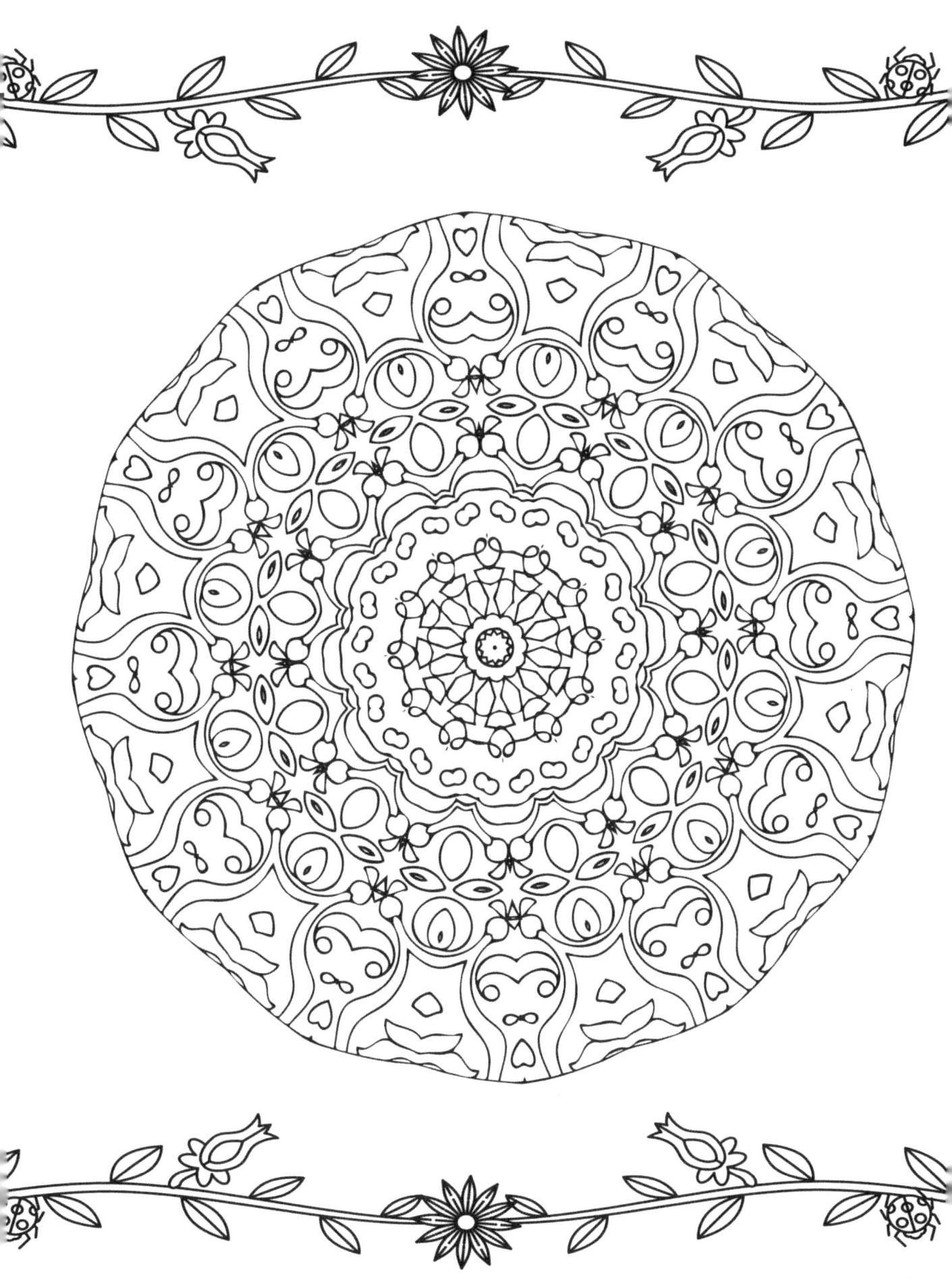

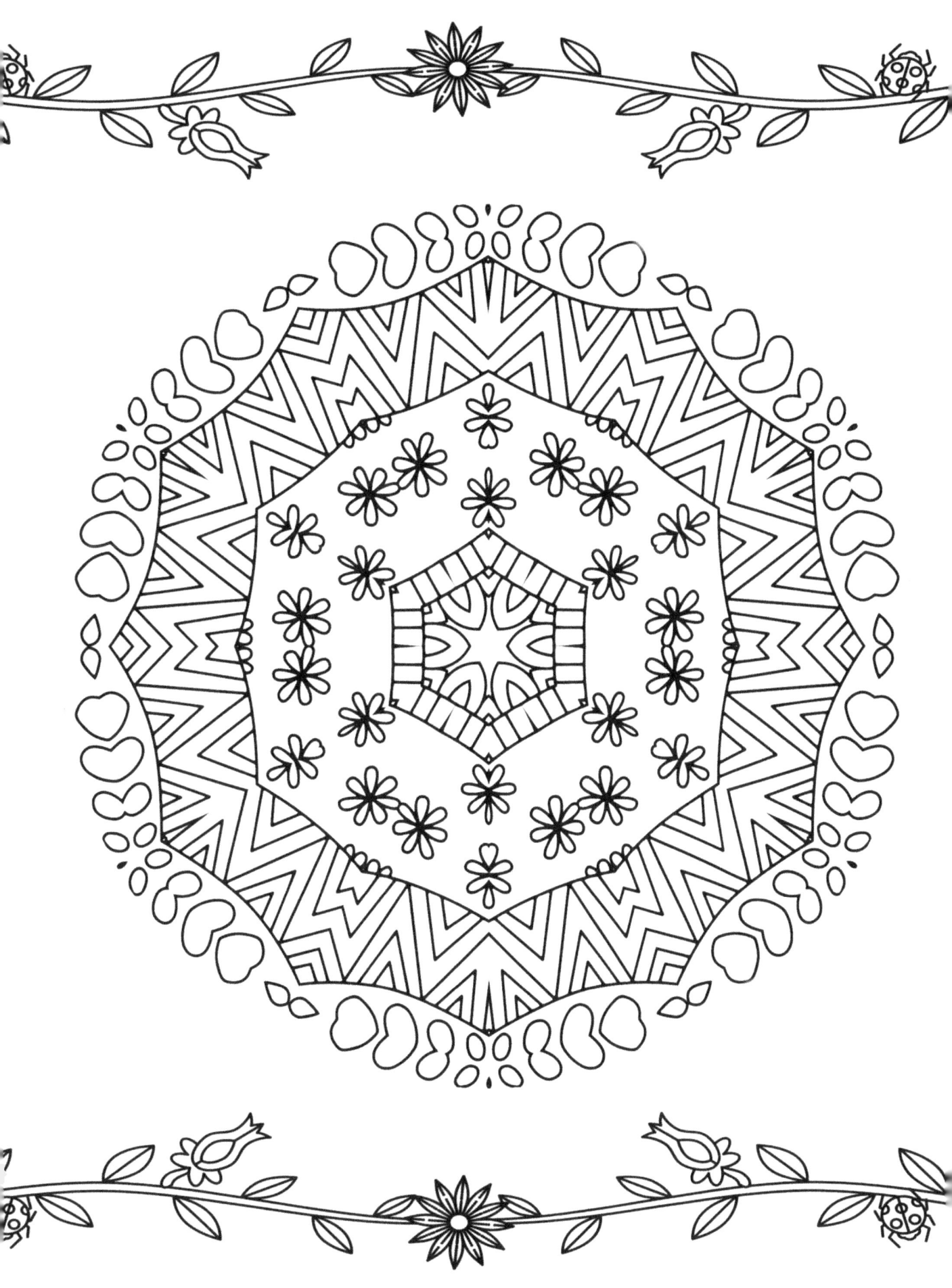

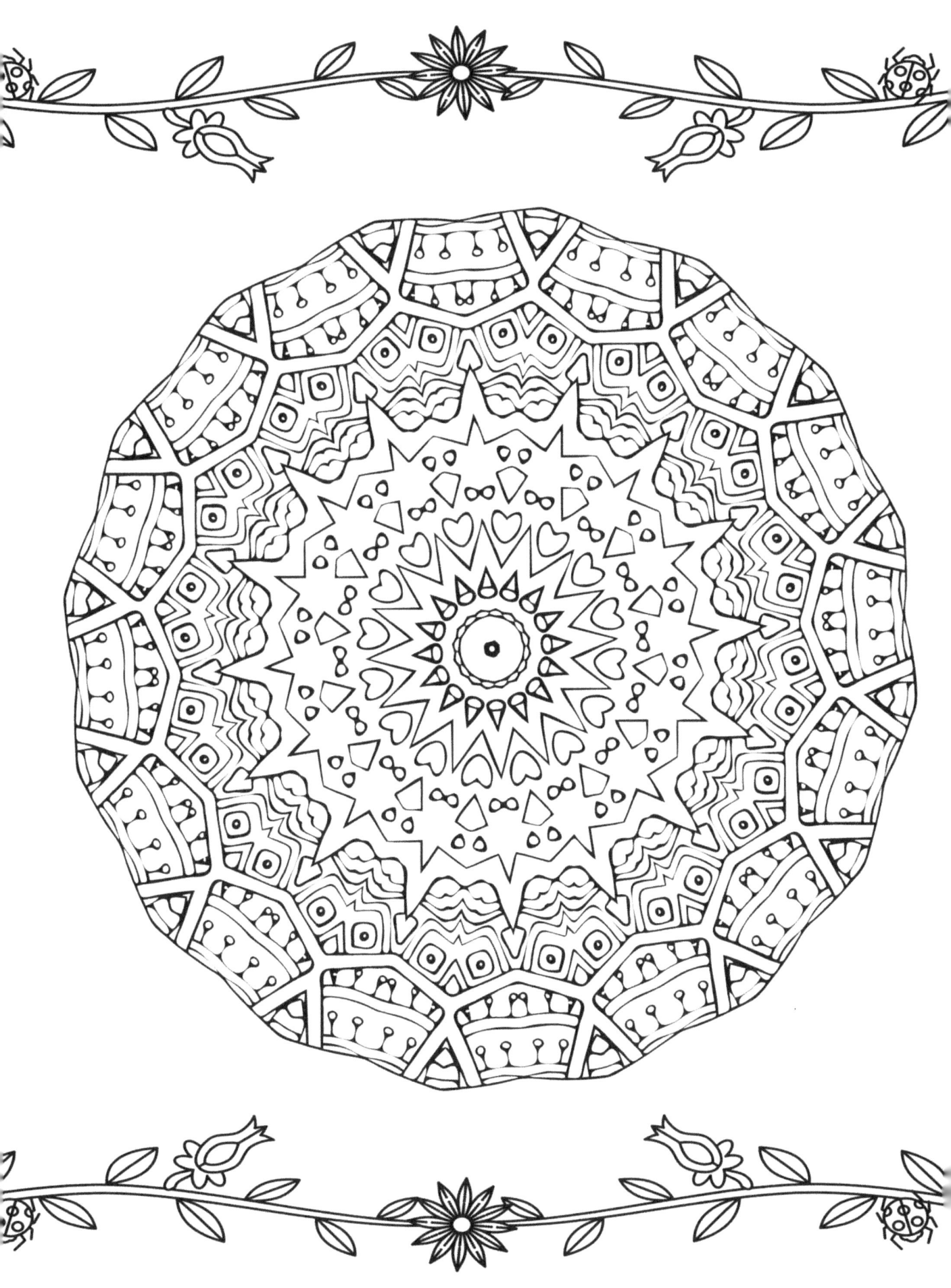

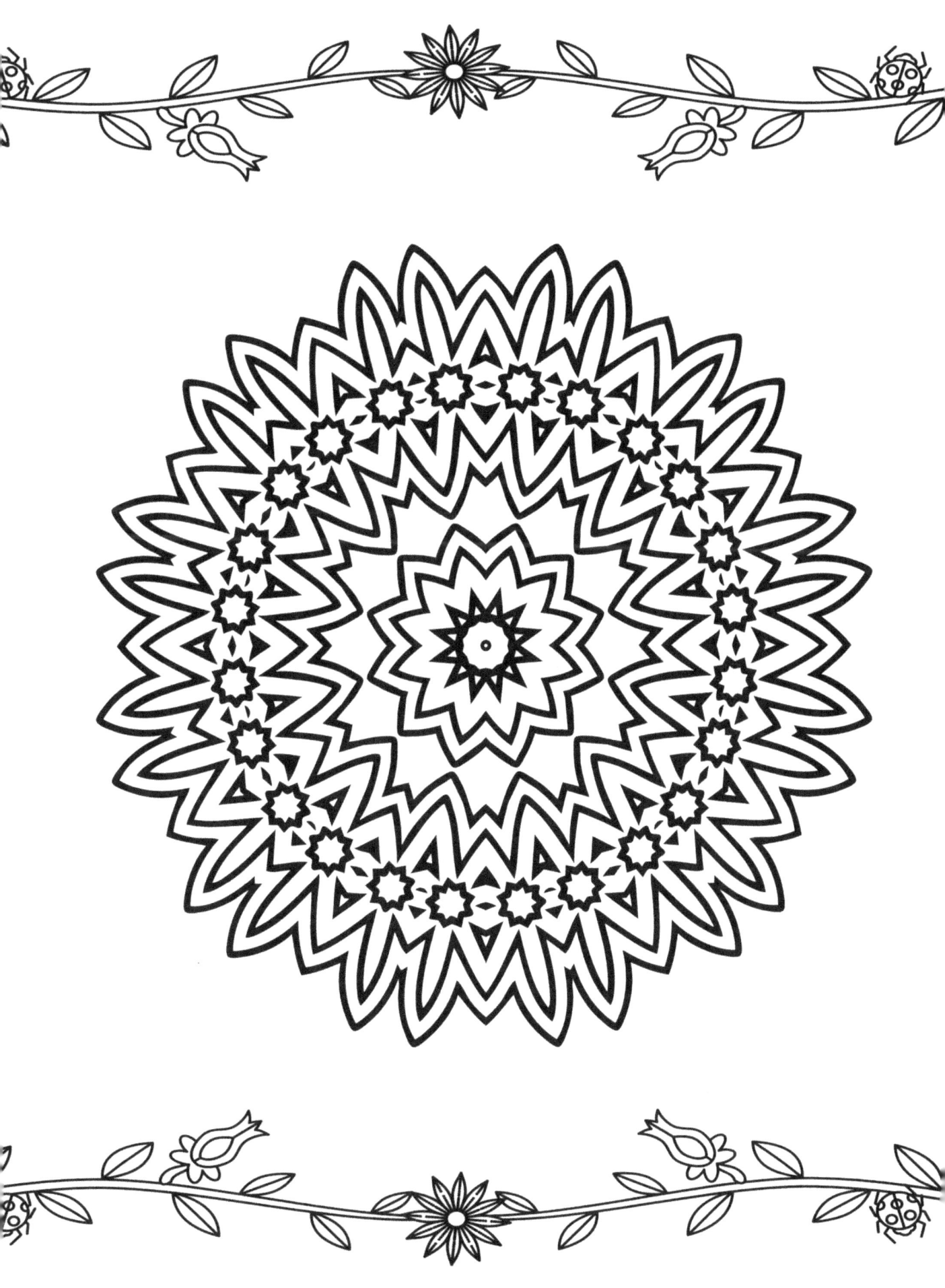

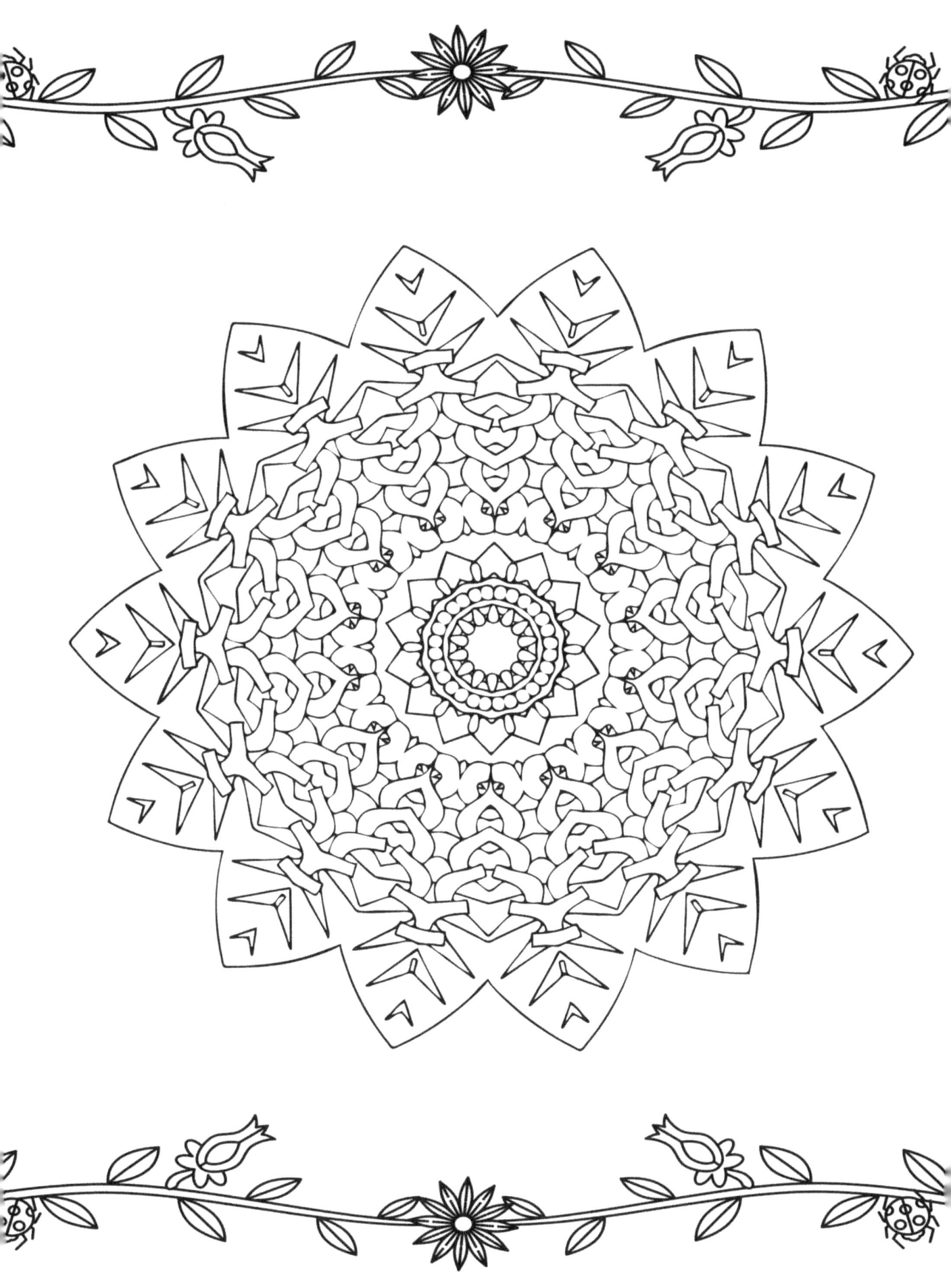

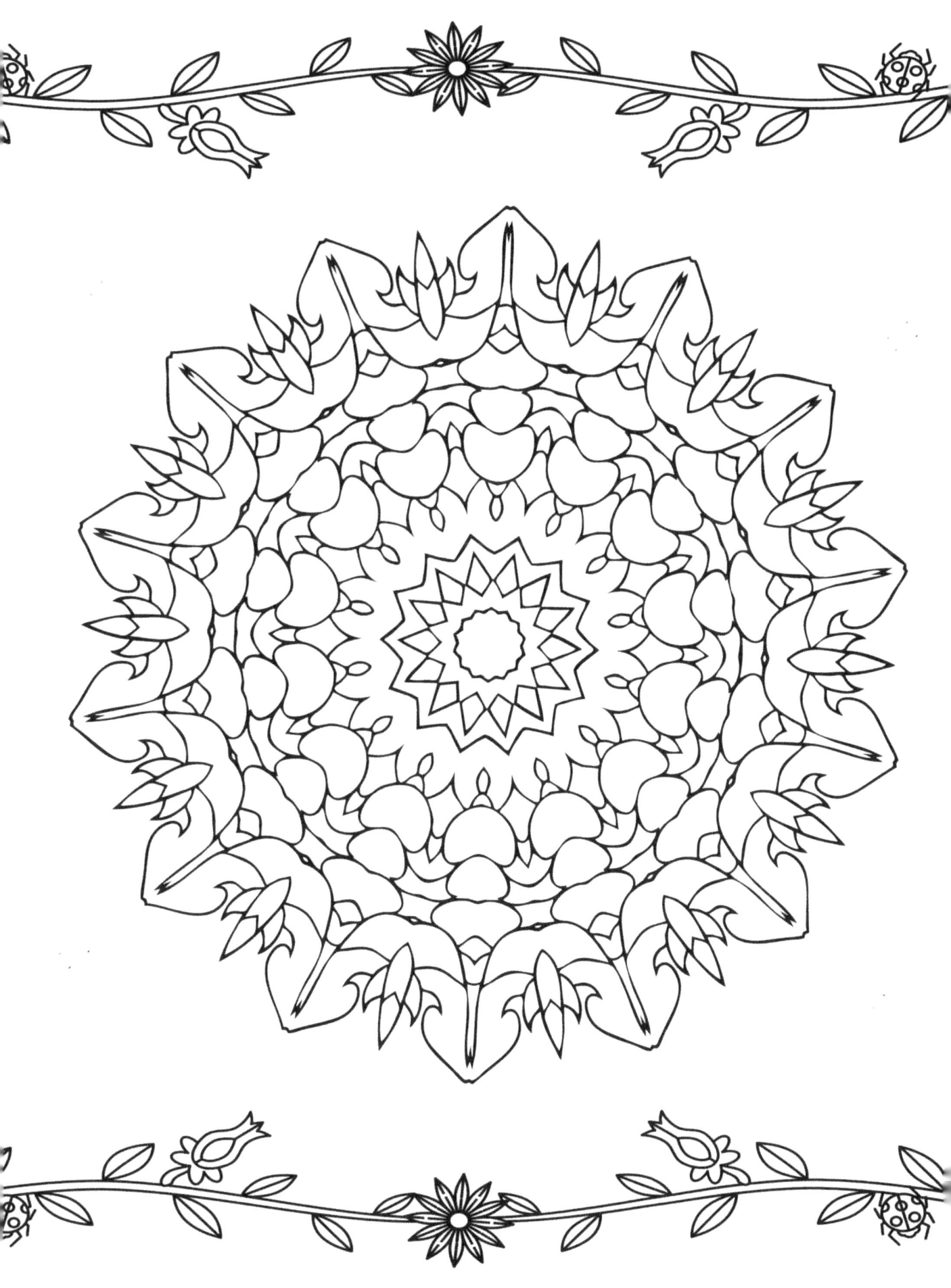

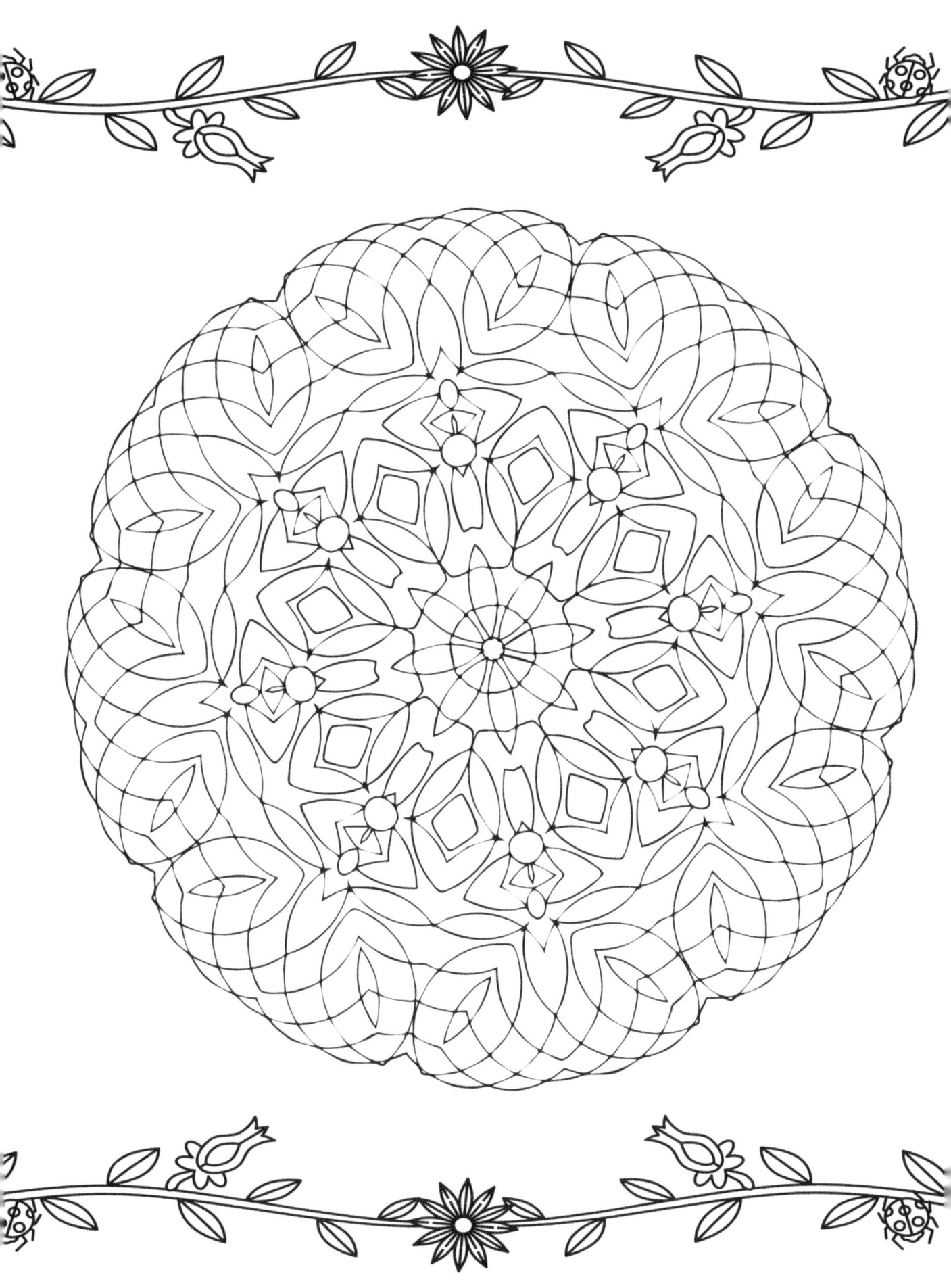

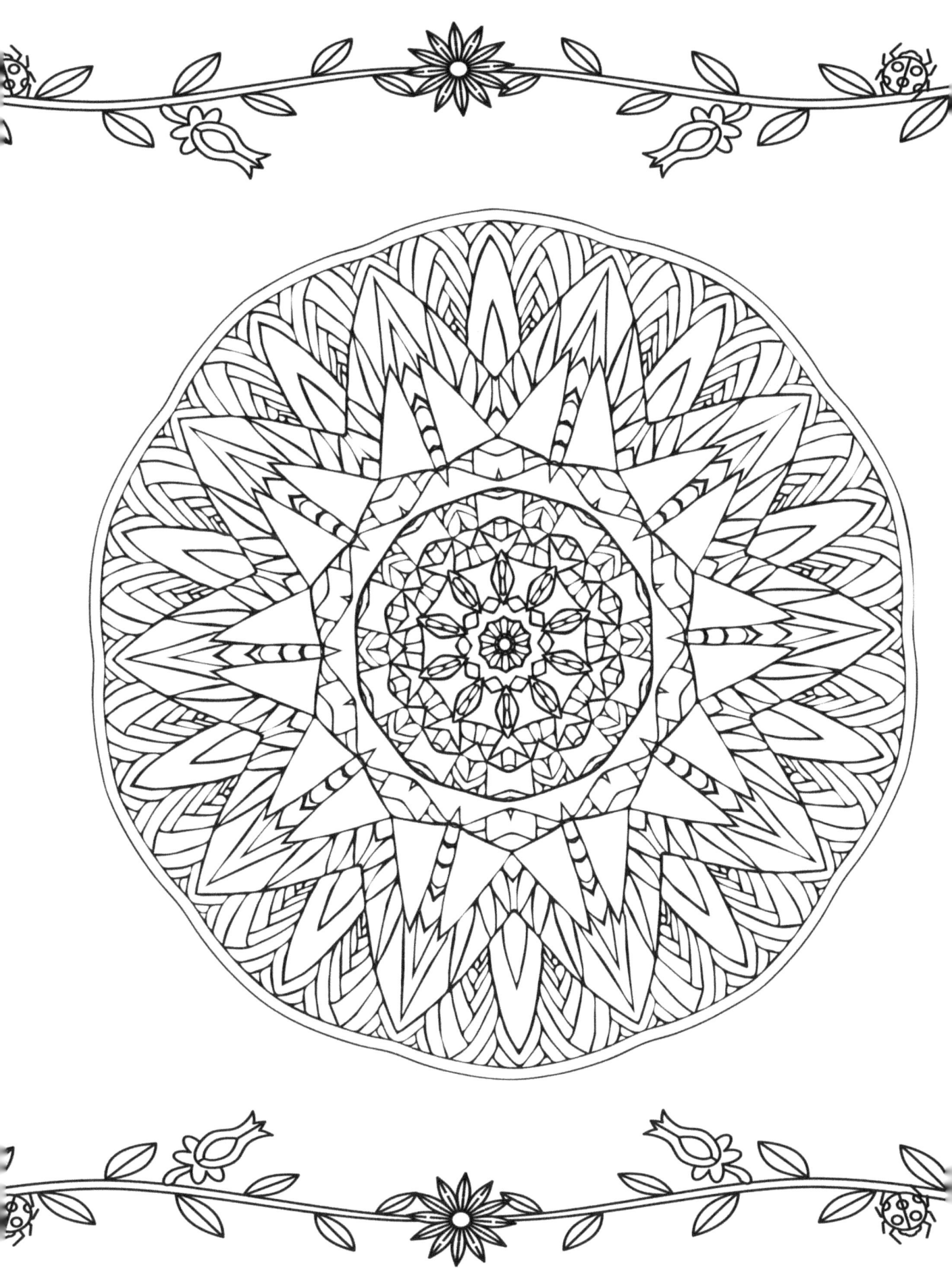

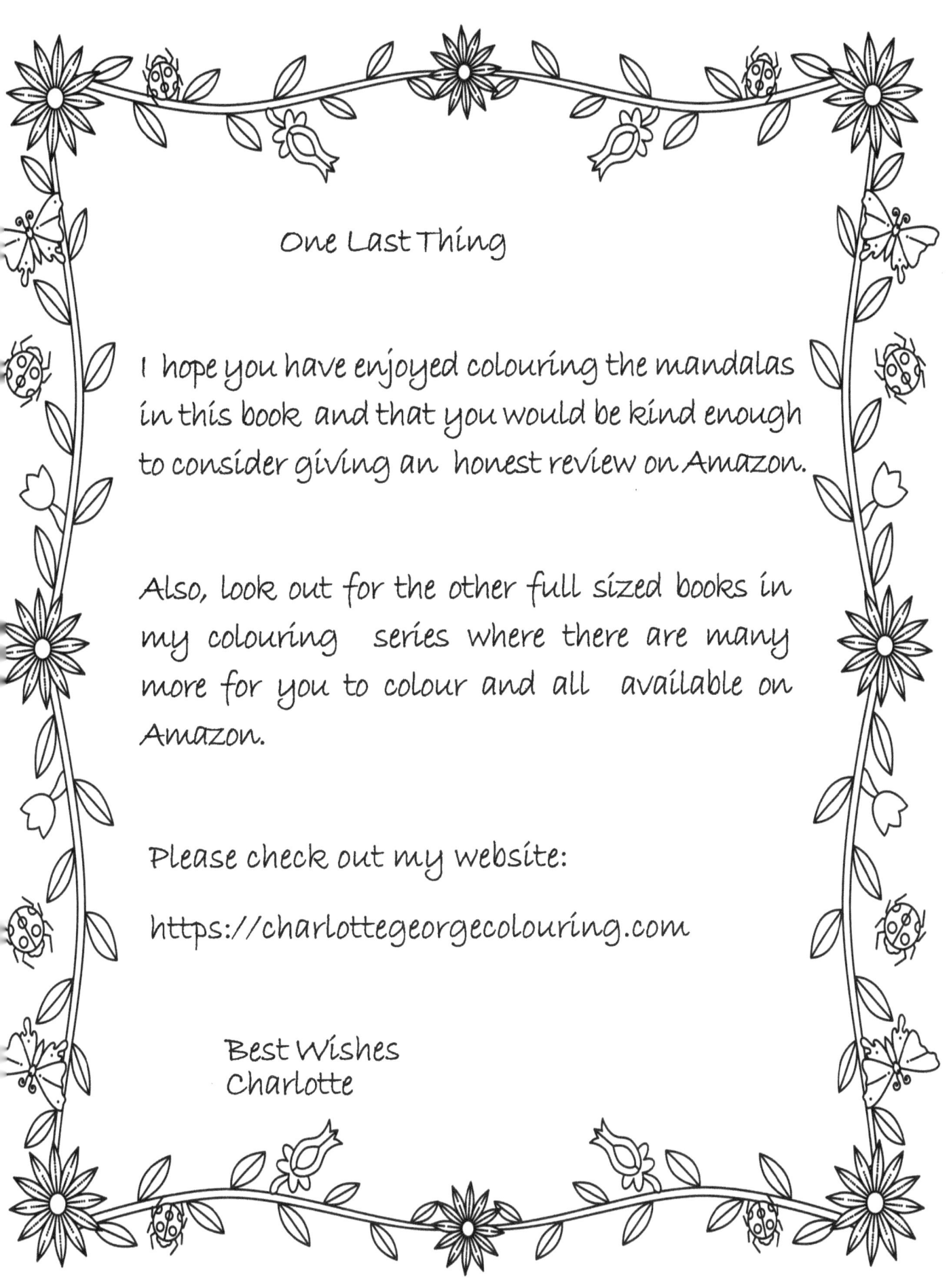

One Last Thing

I hope you have enjoyed colouring the mandalas in this book and that you would be kind enough to consider giving an honest review on Amazon.

Also, look out for the other full sized books in my colouring series where there are many more for you to colour and all available on Amazon.

Please check out my website:

https://charlottegeorgecolouring.com

Best Wishes
Charlotte

www.ingramcontent.com/pod-product-compliance
Lightning Source LLC
Chambersburg PA
CBHW060010210526
45170CB00017B/2137